The Other Night

HERSCHEL FARBMAN

The Other Night

DREAMING, WRITING, AND RESTLESSNESS IN TWENTIETH-CENTURY LITERATURE

Fordham University Press
New York 2008

Library of Congress Cataloging-in-Publication Data

Farbman, Herschel.
The other night : dreaming, writing, and restlessness in twentieth-century literature / Herschel Farbman.
p. cm.
Includes bibliographical references and index.
ISBN 978-0-8232-2865-2 (cloth : alk. paper)
1. Blanchot, Maurice—Criticism and interpretation. 2. Beckett, Samuel, 1906–1989—Criticism and interpretation. 3. Joyce, James, 1882–1941. Finnegans wake. 4. Dreams in literature. I. Title.
PQ2603.L3343Z64 2008
840.9′353—dc22

2008037468

Printed in the United States of America
First paperback printing 2012

for

Evelyn Clark Farbman

and

Marvin Farbman

CONTENTS

ACKNOWLEDGMENTS

Jack Cameron helped me begin to phrase my questions about dreaming and has inspired me with his example. Paul Fry's insights into this project renewed my interest in it and have sustained my work on it. Carol Jacobs' reading of my work has made it more real to me, and her support has allowed me to rethink and revise. Claudine Kahan, Giuseppe Mazzotta, Shoshana Felman, Winfried Menninghaus, John Hamilton, Sandra Naddaff, Geoffrey Hartman, and Marc Shell offered crucial guidance and support at various stages. I am grateful to Catherine Labio, Pericles Lewis, Andrew Parker, and Eyal Peretz for their comments on an earlier version and to Helen Tartar for her galvanizing understanding.

Carolina Sanín's readings of the world have awakened me to my own and to the possibility of imagining my reader as a friend. Tamar Abramov, Molly Breen, Francisca Cabrera, Chinnie Ding, Lance Duerfahrd, Julia Faisst, Daniel Farbman, Melissa Feuerstein, Dan Friedman, Yasco Horsman, Hanneke Grootenboer, Christopher Mason Johnson, Sharon Joyce, Luc Kinsch, Ian Morgan, Molly Murray, Tom Pepper, Eyal Peretz, Ted Rose, Jane Rosenzweig, Karen Schiff, Amina Steinfels, Emmanuel Trouzier, and Jane Unrue have lent ideas and strength.

Amy Powell has been my co-conspirator.

An earlier version of chapter 2 was published in *SubStance* 34, no. 2 (2005).

The Other Night

INTRODUCTION

The Other Night

"I sleep, but my heart wakes"

Every night is two nights, according to Maurice Blanchot. The night of sleep is not the same as the night of the dream. The sleeping body may lie under the stars, and the dreamer may dream of the stars—even of a journey to the stars—but the night of the dream is a night without stars. The dreamer may dream that it's day, but the light in which he or she sees his or her dream is not the light of the sun or of the star of any other world. The world of his or her dream is the world of a night that can never turn to day. According to Blanchot, we sleep because the labor of day—the passing day and the day to come—demands it. The night of sleep belongs to the day. The night of the dream—the night of the unverifiable events of the dream—is another night. Blanchot calls it "the other night."[1] So, even if I wanted to tell you a dream I had last night, I wouldn't be lying, according to Blanchot's rules, if I began the story like this: "The other night I had a dream."

This division of the night in two is Blanchot's way of expressing his sense of the irreducibility of the dream to the sleep on which it depends. According to Blanchot, the dream cannot be understood as a function of sleep (the booming natural science of sleep, spurred by advances in imaging technologies, will thus never capture it).[2] Rather, it represents an extreme restlessness—a resistance to sleep—in the very heart of sleep. Blanchot sometimes calls "the other night" "the heart of the night."[3] The "other night" is not a parallel night nor the night of a parallel world. Rather, it is a sleep-resistant center—an intimate alien—around which the night of sleep curls. The events of the one night cannot be mapped, one-to-one, onto the other. Even with all of the best imaging technology imaginable, the dream cannot be witnessed live by another, whereas sleep can. We can sleep together and we can watch the sleep of another, but we cannot dream together or watch the dream of another. The "other night" is always spent alone, and whether or not Descartes is right that we always dream that we're awake, the "other night" is never spent in sleep, as the dreamer would be no more asleep in a dream of being asleep than he or she is wide awake in a dream of being wide awake.

Because there is no possibility of sleep in the "other night" of the dream, the resistance to sleep that it represents cannot be confused with the waking state in which we spend our days. That state is defined in opposition to the state of sleep. Where there is no possibility of sleep, there can be no waking in this ordinary sense. There is thus no room for philosophical skepticism in Blanchot's account of dreams. However, philosophical skepticism has its roots in a strong sense of the sleeplessness of the dream. Though the skeptic doesn't think of the dream as a form of resistance to sleep, he or she is nagged by worry about how wakeful dream-life can seem. The skeptic translates his or her sense of the sleeplessness of the dream into a worried question about the realism of the dream's representation of waking life: how can I tell the difference between waking and dreaming if I cannot tell the difference between really being awake and my dream's representation of being awake? In philosophical skepticism, the problem of knowing for sure that I'm not dreaming when I'm trying to know something by light of day is the problem of telling the difference between a representation and what it represents—between true waking and its forgery. Framed this way, the problem is famously intractable.

As Blanchot frames the problem, the difference between the waking we do by day and our sleeplessness in dreams can be told, though certainly not in such a way as to give anyone any rest. A difference that cannot be told in terms of true versus false can be told as a tale of two truths. Where the philosophical skeptic, certain only that he or she is deceived in feeling that there is something sleepless about dreams, tries to make out the difference between true vigilance and an imitation, Blanchot sees two distinct but not strictly opposed kinds of true vigilance. One kind—the kind characteristic of the vigil we keep by day—is defined in opposition to sleep and ceases the moment sleep begins. The other underlies the ordinary opposition between sleep and waking and appears as resistance to sleep in the heart of sleep, sheer difference from sleep, an impossibility of complete sleep opening up in the depths of sleep and creating in sleep the internal boundary that makes it possible. Within life, there is no sleep deeper than the ordinary sleep we fall in and out of, no sleep as deep as this underlying vigilance. The only sleep deeper than the one that comes and goes is the sleep our lives are rounded with.

Complete sleep would be death. To see our sleeplessness in dreams as real in the way that Blanchot urges is not to deny that it is fundamentally a matter of images but rather to recognize these images as signs of life. Dream-images deceive us in imitating the waking life that gives way every night to sleep, but in their very unfolding, these same images also testify to a waking that doesn't give way—the ongoing movement by which sleep, death's portrait, can be differentiated with certainty from death. In its self-reflexive expression of its own movement, the dream is not the kind of illusion of waking life that the philosophical skeptic takes it to be. It is not the sort of fiction that might be opposed to a reality and substituted for it by mistake. Rather, it is a face of the supreme fiction on which the real difference between life and death rests. The *1001 Nights*, in which Scheherazade's stories keep the sultan awake and, in keeping the sultan awake, keep the storyteller alive, can be read as an allegory of the death-deferring function that dreaming performs every night, for everyone. Seen as a version of waking life, dream-life is imaginary. Waking life ends where sleep begins. But because the dream itself resists sleep from within, real life—life itself—does not end where waking life ends. In Blanchot's "other night," the alternate reality that the dream represents opens up not in the form of a parallel world that might be confused with this one but in the alien heart of the night of sleep.

So, by distinguishing between the reality of the "other night" (the starless night into which the imaging technologies of sleep science cannot penetrate) and the reality of the night of sleep (the starlit night in which the sleeping body lies, open to view, scientific and otherwise), Blanchot is able to describe the dream as a kind of nocturnal waking without falling into skeptical confusions about the difference between this waking and the kind of waking we do by day. Distinctive though it is, this distinction is not Blanchot's alone. Since the first appearance of ancient skepticism, skeptical worry has certainly been the most common way in which the sleeplessness of the dream has been felt, both in and out of philosophy—Calderón's *Life Is a Dream* is the exemplar in literature, and ordinary talk about dreams often follows these same lines—but breaking with this old tradition, Blanchot falls in with another one.

"I sleep, but my heart wakes," says the *Song of Songs* (5:2). Where Blanchot distinguishes between the night of sleep and "the heart of the night," the *Song of Songs* distinguishes between the "I" who sleeps and his or her sleepless heart. In both cases, a heart is the organ of the resistance to sleep that distinguishes the dream from ordinary waking life. The waking heart changes shape—what had been the agent of the dream in the *Song of Songs* becomes its open site in Blanchot—but it remains sworn to this resistance. Indeed, it could not serve this cause if it were bound to any fixed form. Its resistance to the rule of day—to the sleep that gathers forces for the work of day—must remain underground. The movement essential to the organ is that by which it guards itself from open view, showing itself only in ever-shifting forms and locations. Such a heart cannot be laid bare. Laid bare it would cease to be. The story of the tradition of the non-skeptical manner of experiencing the sleeplessness of the dream is a story of the transformations to which the waking heart is given from the very moment of its awakening.

This book is about a relatively recent episode in this story. Freud and Joyce—the subjects of the first and last chapters of this book—wrote their epoch-defining dreambooks just the other night, relatively speaking.

The Interpretation of Dreams and *Finnegans Wake* bookend an age of big modernist projects, many of which—from Proust's *Recherche* to surrealism to Benjamin's unfinished *Arcades Project*—make the dream a central concern. Both Freud and Joyce articulate experiences of waking in the very depths of sleep, where no "I" can declare itself present though the heart still beats. After World War II, in the cold light of the closure of the age of dreambooks, Beckett and Blanchot—the subjects of the middle chapters of this book—discover with new clarity, and new fatigue, that what wakes when the "I" sleeps doesn't sleep when the "I" wakes. Restless night stretches on after night.

There are 1001 nights of the story of the movements of the waking heart before Freud takes up the tale, and each night can be told as a story within another. Let me quickly embed the night of this book in two others: the night of the heart that wakes in the songs of the troubadours and the night that Don Quixote descends into in descending into a cave that Cervantes locates "in the heart of La Mancha."[4]

The Heart in the "Heart of La Mancha"

The movement of the heart in the sleeper's chest continues unbroken throughout the stillness of the night of sleep. The heart is the most restless of organs. Or, if it is not really the most restless of organs, it is the organic symbol of the restlessness of mortal life. When the dream is felt as resistance to the stillness of sleep—felt as evidence of an ongoing movement underlying all of the movements of day and continuing throughout the stillness of the night—then it is natural, as it were, that an association between the dream and the onward-beating heart be felt. The *Song of Songs* is a very early song of this underlying movement that, though it is ceaseless, is most vividly felt in stillness. In the first songs composed in the vernaculars of medieval Europe, this ongoing movement is expressed in a new conjunction of thoughts about dreaming. "I sleep, but my heart wakes" translates to "I sleep, and therefore poetry occurs to me."

In this new kind of song in which the night belongs to lovers who lie dreamily awake until the arrival of the dream-dispersing dawn, the movement by which the dream resists collapse into sleep is felt as the movement by which verse is discovered. The figure of the knight who sleeps in the saddle and, in sleeping, discovers a poem is well-traveled in the medieval world.[5] The first troubadour, Guillaume of Aquitaine, is already at play with it: "I will make a verse about nothing / . . . for it was found while I was sleeping / on horseback."[6] Otherwise hidden by day, the movement of the sleepless heart—the heart that is given to the other and awaits the other in the new songs of love—is traced by the movement of the horse and by the verses, discovered in sleep, that the rider delivers (often to one of several further intermediaries) once he has arrived at whatever court his horse was heading to. In his song, he circulates a letter from his sleepless heart, posted in the depths of sleep.

Like the first practitioners of courtly love, the belated Don Quixote dreams of writing. But whereas the troubadours find new writing in their dreams, Don Quixote dreams of the romances he has read. In both cases, the lover's heart is the organ of the dream, but the cardiology of the cases differs. In medieval dream-writing, the heart is idealized. Flesh becomes word. In Don Quixote's errant dream of the literature of knights errant, the words he has read become flesh. The ironic result of Cervantes's comic treatment of this central trope of Christian book-culture is that the heart is returned to the body from which it is symbolically removed in the medieval discourse of love, dreaming, and writing. However, Cervantes doesn't leave it there, broken as a symbol, never to dream again. Instead, he pushes the irony further.

In the center of Cervantes's book—in a cave located by the chapter heading in "the heart of La Mancha"—Don Quixote has what all indices strongly suggest is a dream, though he himself reports it as a waking vision.[7] In the dream, he sees another knight—Durandarte, a great medieval precursor—lying prone, as if asleep. According to the chivalric romance, Durandarte, defeated and dying, commands his friend, Montesinos, to cut out his heart upon his death and take it to his beloved Belerma. In Don Quixote's modern dream, his precursor is magically still alive, despite the hole in his chest. Thus the terms of the medieval knight's gesture are ironically reversed "in the heart of La Mancha." In the medieval romance, Durandarte gives his heart, in death, to his beloved to demonstrate that his love, which his heart symbolizes, lives on. The body dies but the signifying heart lives on. In the revisionism of Don Quixote's dream, the knight lives on, though prone as if in sleep, with a chest as hollow as the cave into which Don Quixote has been lowered. His heart, however, is subject to rot like any other meat. Montesinos says he had to salt it. Likewise, he has to apologize for the appearance of its recipient, Belerma, who turns out to be nearly as ugly as Don Quixote's Dulcinea.

These revelations would seem to be thoroughly demystifying, and yet the more realistic Don Quixote's vision of the heart of romance becomes, the more marvelous it all comes to seem to him. When, in the cruelest moment of the comedy of the dream in the cave, Dulcinea asks Don Quixote for money, his rapt wonder at the vision only deepens. And Don Quixote's wonder must be, to a large extent, our own. The only thing we see that he doesn't (because we see only what he tells us that he sees) is that he has, very likely, been dreaming. There's a good joke on Don Quixote in this dramatic irony, but because Don Quixote's vision already includes its own satire, the joke does not make a mockery of the vision. To remark that the vision is "just a dream" is only to underline a profound *mise en abîme.* Looking at the prone body of the knight, Don Quixote looks at an image of himself, asleep. And looking into the knight's grotesquely hollowed-out chest, Don Quixote looks at an image of the space of his own dream—the cave in "the heart of La Mancha."

The grand discourse of chivalric romance is hollow at its heart. Cervantes's satire does indeed insist on this. But the hollow space that the satire reveals in its comic literalization of the figure of the gift of the heart is not a void. Cervantes's satire does not void the gift but rather opens up a way of contemplating the very possibility of having a heart to give in the first place. By doubling the figure of the lover's gift of his heart back upon itself, Cervantes gives a cardiogram of a real heart of hearts—not an idealized, symbolic organ within the real organ but the real space that echoes in the ironies of the organ's comically compulsive symbolic absence. To call this space "heart" is to speak figuratively—to transfer the name of the organ to a space—but the heart is an essentially transferential organ, and every transference of the heart implies the opening of a heart of hearts, offering, in the process, an opening to satire.

The Space of Dreams, Open Space of Literature

The cave "in the heart of La Mancha" is not exactly the same space as Blanchot's "heart of the night." Some sun filters into the cave, and there's nothing in Blanchot quite like the rope by which Don Quixote is lowered into the cave by his companions and by which he remains connected, throughout the episode, to the world of day. But in both cases "heart" names the space in which a dream takes place. Cervantes's romantic satire on romance tells the tale of the opening of this space.

It might seem that the fast advancing brain science of dreaming would have rendered the study of this "heart" obsolete. New imaging technologies are producing newly vivid images of the activity of the brain in sleep. It is tempting to view these images as improved representations of the same activity that, seen through a glass darkly, had looked like the movements of the waking heart. That is, it is tempting to fill the space of the heart with the brain. However, the operation can't work. To substitute scientific images of nocturnal brain activity for the old images of the waking heart is as aberrant a metaphorical procedure as any medieval displacement of the heart ever was. The new images of the activity of the brain in sleep are beautiful pictures of the night of sleep and of the dream seen from the perspective of this night, but they give no picture of the dream seen as a dream. The better the scientific imaging gets, the clearer it becomes that we will never be able to see a dream in it. No scientist will ever be able to tell what his or her experimental subject dreamed from the images of the brain activity of that subject in sleep.

Only the dreamer can see his or her dream, and only the dreamer can tell its tale. No one can corroborate or contest the dreamer's tale. As Freud recognized, the question of whether or not it really happened that way has to be suspended in assessing the truth of the dream-tale.[8] Thus only fiction—"fiction" naming here that genre- and media-crossing discourse of strange facts that don't require corroboration to be credited—will ever be able to represent the space that opens up behind the closed eyes of the sleeper. And because fiction has a special right to this space, this is where it lives. The house of fiction is the house of dreams. In entering dreams, everyone enters, every night, an experience the facts of which cannot be corroborated by anyone else.

It's because dream-tales cannot be corroborated—because only the dreamer can see and tell his or her dream—that, as Keats says in the proem to *The Fall of Hyperion: A Dream,* "Poesy alone can tell her dreams" (line 8). ("Poesy" is a rosier name for what I've just called "fiction"; let's call it "poetry," to use a no less thorny but more common name.) Keats condenses two contrary thoughts in this formulation. One thought aggrandizes poetry: it's only in poetry that dreams can be told, and therefore only poets can truly tell dreams. The other casts poetry as one dreamer among others, subject to the common rule that no dreamer is able to tell the dream of another. The condensation of these two thoughts is a function of cohabitation—it happens because poetry lives in the house of dreams. Not every dreamer is a poet, but every poet must be a dreamer. Thus a separation between the tribe of poets and the tribe of dreamers cannot be as cleanly made as Moneta, the muse, tries to make it when she tells the dreamer/poet of *The Fall of Hyperion* that he is but a dreamer.[9] And because every poet must be a dreamer, no dreamer but the muse herself, who has a divine right to be wrong, has the right to tell another that he or she is not a poet: "Who alive can say / Thou art no Poet—mayst not tell thy dreams?" (lines 11–12).

Telling dreams calls for poetry, everyone has dreams to tell, and no one can tell the dream of another. Most dreams thus go untold, as, in fact, not everyone is a poet, and even poets like Keats and the Coleridge of *Kubla Khan,* who have ventured far into the telling of their dreams, discover that the telling can't be complete—that the story that ends up getting told in the telling of a dream is always the story of the loss involved in the telling. A telling of a dream cannot be a poetic success without producing pathos about the loss of the dream—a sense of the "pity these have not / Traced upon vellum or wild Indian leaf / The shadows of melodious utterance" (lines 4–6)—and a dream cannot be truly told if the telling is not a poetic success. Even if, as Lautréamont wished, poetry were made by everyone—even if everyone were a poet—the better part of dreams would go untold and, with this loss, poetry would feel that it was losing its better part.[10] This part of the dream destined for loss is the heart of poetry.

The story of the loss of this heart can always be told as a love story. Like Cervantes, Blanchot tells it this way (though with both less satire and less romance). Where Cervantes rewrites the story of Durandarte and Belerma, Blanchot rewrites the story of Orpheus and Eurydice. The inevitable loss to poetry of its heart is told—in the center (the heart) of *The Space of Literature* and throughout Blanchot's work—as the necessary turn by which Eurydice is lost.[11] By this turn and the loss it entails the "space of literature" is opened up in "the heart of the night." The space in the heart of the literary oeuvre is a space hollowed out by the great "*absence d'oeuvre*" of the world—by the loss that both calls for telling and exceeds it. The "heart of the night" is the hollow space in time in which literature is born and to which it returns, every night, dissolving the work of day and all of its worldly distinctions—including the distinction between poet and non-poet—into the dark of "the other night" that everyone enters unwitnessed, every night, in dreams.

Unrest, Literary and Democratic

This book is in search of the current coordinates of this nocturnal meeting place where the poet, stripped of laurels, encounters the non-poet in him or herself and finds, in this encounter, both the inspiration and the undoing of his or her work. Here the poet joins everyone else not as the representative of everyone else but on common ground. Everyone dreams. No one meets anyone else in dreams—everyone is equally alone in the experience of his or her dreams—but everyone is subject to this experience for which no one else, not even the most powerfully representative poet, can speak and in which even the most powerful poet encounters the limits of his or her powers of speech. This book argues that this nightly experience that can't be shared is an experience of language as shared—of the sharing of language—and that the experience is essentially literary. According to Freud's theory, in which this argument is rooted, the images of the dream, which seem to represent things, in fact represent words. That is, they constitute, in his words, "a pictographic script."[12] Every dreamer—everyone, literate or not, poet or not—is involved in a form of writing.

"Here Comes Everybody," says Joyce, pointing to the irreducible multiplicity of one of the central characters (HCE) of *Finnegans Wake*, Joyce's still only partly mapped exploration of the kind of waking that goes on even in the depths of sleep. And along with Everybody comes a general unrest in literature. The great dreambooks of the first half of the twentieth century throw open the doors of literature to a general unrest by their insistence that the cohabitation of dream and writing is not just a question of a certain oneiric style. Literature lives in the house of dreams, no longer in the form of this or that dream-inspired or dream-dictated work, but in the written form of everyone's every dream. In the immediate aftermath of the age of dreambooks, Blanchot and Beckett make unrest a major theme. The restlessness that they report is so extreme, and their sense of it is so refined, that it is easy to miss its democratic implications. But there is nothing exclusive about the opening they point to in the restless heart of the night.

The nocturnal meeting place, the opening I'm looking for in this book, cannot be too far from a graveyard. It's in the graveyard that sleep looks most like death and there that it pays most to know the difference (the difference being the dream, eternal enemy of eternal rest). Had Romeo only known better the difference—had he only wanted to know it better—he would not have become a tragic hero but rather would have departed the tomb of the Capulets a survivor, a teller of something like *A Midsummer Night's Dream.* The graveyard is also, and not coincidentally, a privileged place for thoughts of radical equality, the particular and particularly uneasy political cause I want to link here to a conception of the dream as a form of unease. Even at times when thoughts of equality have no place in the city, no bearing on political life, the king is expected to say "we're all equal here" when he visits the graveyard. Of course, the graveyard that calls for this thought can also swallow it up before it leads to any action. Equal in death does not imply equal in life. An impossible translation between the two would be necessary. That translation would be democracy—a dream. For now, the area between the two—the region of dreams—remains gray, gray like the shifty, self-burying author of the graveyard poem of graveyard poems, Gray's *Elegy Written in a Country Churchyard.*

The Gray Area of Writing

Gray's *Elegy* is not a poem of dreams—at least not explicitly—but, written on the eve of modern democracy, it is perhaps the first poem in which the loss of the lives of those who "rest in unvisited tombs"[13] is lamented as, among other things, lost writing. Gray wonders about the writing that might have been done but wasn't by those buried in the country churchyard. "Mute inglorious Miltons" (line 59)—Miltons mute and inglorious because of the injustice of the world and its accidents of birth—may lie there. By the end of his *Elegy*, Gray has himself lying dead in their place and uttering his own epitaph from the space of muteness, in the person of a mute inglorious Milton himself. In this act of projective self-burial, Gray throws into real disarray all straightforward conceptions of the relationship between those who write and those who don't, writing and not writing, the literary work and the great *absence d'oeuvre* of the world—between the sweet nothings that make it into poetry and all of the untold dreams and thoughts of all of the unrepresented subjects of history.

Nothing loses itself to history like a dream. As we've seen, a poem of dreams is a poem of loss. Often it's a kind of graveyard poem. The dreamer-poet feels the dream on the tip of his or her tongue and chases it, again and again, into the muteness and ingloriousness of Gray's pre-romantic graveyard. Trying to get at the feeling, the poet contorts him or herself into the same strange posture toward writing that doesn't get done that Gray buries himself in at the end of his *Elegy*. The poet feels the loss of a dream as a loss of *writing*—the loss not necessarily of paradise but perhaps of a *Paradise Lost*. The dream makes the poet a Milton but leaves him or her mute. The troubadours found works of writing in their dreams, and, by the same token—a token passed quietly from pocket to pocket, dream to dream, from the twelfth century to modern times—writers, like Coleridge in *Kubla Khan*, have felt that they lost writing in forgetting their dreams. The sense of this loss can take a thousand forms. In *Kubla Khan*, the lost poem itself seems to have been a poem of loss—the dream a dream of its own forgetting. Perhaps there's an ironic gain in this loss of loss, or perhaps the loss is just doubly painful. Whatever literary gains there may be in it, it's in the nature of this loss that it can't be properly mourned. The object lost—the dream as literary work—is lost because it never really becomes an object. There's nothing there to bury, and the writer will thus bury him or herself, Gray-like, in place of his or her dream-writing. If it ever can be produced sufficiently for proper burial, this lost object can only be seen as such when, as Keats says at the end of the proem to *The Fall of Hyperion,* the poet is in the grave—when "this warm scribe, this hand, is in the grave" (line 18).

There is no graveyard of lost dreams, no place of monuments to all of the writing that never was done. A little graveyard of the kind sketched by Gray is still the place—the common if not exactly public place—to which thoughts of that loss displace themselves. They go there more to die—to bury themselves in melancholy—than to be acted upon. William Empson and John Guillory have powerfully shown (in very different ways) how anxiety about undone writing buries itself in Gray's *Elegy* before it can be converted to action.[14] But the anxiety buried there is buried alive, and it will remain alive there until the glorious revolution in which no dream will go unrecorded, no Milton will be mute, and no talent will be wasted. All of the world's restlessness, the essential stuff of dreams, is preserved in this writing anxiety, this objectless worry (worry about all of the writing that doesn't take objective form). To feel this anxiety is to have a feeling for the political sense it might make to speak of writing beyond this or that work, writing in or as *absence d'oeuvre*—to talk that kind of nonsense about writing. There's method beyond evasive maneuvering in the mad (and maddeningly calm) morbidity of Gray's graveyard poet.

The central and most slippery maneuver of this strangely popular and enduring poem by an otherwise largely forgotten poet is well known, well loved, and much hated. The poet, wracked with something like what Barbara Johnson calls "muteness envy," expresses it by leaping, like Hamlet but without any of the fight, into the grave of the mute inglorious Milton he pretends to mourn.[15] And there he stays. In the magic of a staggering turn of figurative speech, a mute inglorious Milton speaks—speaks his own epitaph—from the grave at the end of Gray's *Elegy*. Glorious ingloriousness. But Gray's magic is at least a little black. It all feels a little like grave robbery, a sneaky, roundabout way for Gray to don the dark mantles Milton used in *Lycidas* to perform a similar trick, whereby a learned mourner becomes an "uncouth swain" in a bizarre final twist.[16] The trick—full of wild projections of the poet's frustrated desires—is more than a little insulting to the nameless subjects it's performed upon.

And sensitive critics like William Empson have responded to this insult with outrage.

But how can insult be avoided in regrets over someone's unrealized potential when these are expressed after the point of realizing any of it is past? An unjust "system" may be entirely to blame for this or that waste of talent, but it's still a person's life and accomplishments you're talking about. Such speech cannot but hurt. Nonetheless, I think there may be deeper injury in avoiding this sort of insult than there is in voicing it. Can the graveyard poet feel the accident of his birth, the contingency of his own poem, the injustice in which he and it are born without blurting out such backhanded compliments? The commonplace that we are all equal in death, that "the paths of glory lead but to the grave" (Gray, line 36), is the place in language to which the poet of the accident of birth and the injustice of the world must go. There can be no sense of the accident of birth independent of a sense of the common necessity of death. The graveyard toward which we are headed from birth is hardly a place of freedom from the slings and arrows of outrageous fortune. Rather, it's the place where the outrageousness of fortune makes itself most hauntingly clear.

In the outrageous desire that it expresses to speak *from* such a common place and not only about it, Gray's *Elegy Written in a Country Churchyard* is bound to be outrageous and insulting. The poet is no peasant and thus can't know of what he speaks. That's fortune for you. But, if the poem isn't a pure outrage—if some real outrage at the injustice of the world is carried in its melancholic drift—it's because the poet does express some true knowledge about where he's writing from when he claims to write from a country churchyard, though he doesn't know of what he speaks, doesn't really know what's buried there. He knows he writes, ultimately, from a place of muteness in himself and that this place is a commonplace—an unavoidable entanglement in language—and not the contingent social place that good fortune has assigned him. The appearance of his poem is, like any birth, a historical accident, but the place it comes from is not the social place into which the poet is born but the commonplace he enters upon death. There has to be something true in this story for there to be any poetry in the poem's outrageous drowning of outrage in melancholia.

The historicism that has dominated the past twenty years of literary criticism has taught us, rightly, to be suspicious of this sort of story. Writing emerges in social contexts and constitutes a form of action in and upon those contexts. In claiming to occupy, at the end of his poem, the space of the "mute inglorious Miltons," Gray anxiously refuses to take up a firm position within the relations of the production of his own poem. The historicist story brings into vivid relief the social character of the anxiety that makes Gray's *Elegy* such an endlessly shifty read. This is illuminating. But this fundamental gesture of historicism can quickly become obscurantist. It's not easy to bring the contingent, social character of a text's anxieties into relief without, at the same time, falsely promising and falsely feeling relief from those anxieties. The claim of historical perspective can easily become smug and serve to remove readers from the real historical dirt in which texts like Gray's *Elegy* really do bury them. Can we give a less shifty description of the place from which we write about Gray than Gray could give of the place from which his *Elegy* is written?

Even if we could determine with certainty the production site where Gray first committed his *Elegy* to the page—even if we could know for sure whether it happened, as Gray says it does, in a country churchyard or at a nice oak desk in a well-appointed room—and even if we knew every detail of the history by which Gray's manuscript first made it to press, we wouldn't thereby have determined the real location from which it emerges. Writing is not just committing black ink to a white page—here with pens, there with presses. The real location from which it emerges is a Grayer area, historically speaking, than most historicism can admit. Here the blind lead the blind, and Gray remains as good a guide as one can find as one tries to feel one's way, in writing, toward a fair sense of the real historical contours of the place. Contextualist reading approaches that place as a place of origin—historical contexts are always defined by circumscribing, whether broadly or narrowly, a time and place of origin—and it replaces the figure of the originating genius with figures (often problematic personifications, i.e. "the stories Elizabethan culture tells itself") of the social and cultural forces at work in the production of a text. This way of approaching questions of origin can account for much that ahistoricist criticism cannot sufficiently account for in literary texts (for example, the historical contingency of the conditions of a text's production). But contextualist reading can't see that the place from which writing emerges is as much a place of death as it is a production site.

Death is a break in the circumscribing logic of social contexts. It has a social side—it has its industries and institutions and a cemetery, like a city, has rich neighborhoods and poor neighborhoods—but dying, leaving the party, is a deeply asocial thing to do. Hamlet and Gray and all of the other purveyors of the clichés of graveyard wisdom notice something true when they note, whether with a gasp or a sigh, the disappearance of social distinctions in death. Though always reached alone, our end is common. The assertion, always true enough, that the author is not made immortal by his or her art—that his or her art is historical and not eternal—seems, in returning the author to history, to gesture toward the commonness of our common end. But the completion of the gesture requires some acknowledgment that the experience of death is essentially asocial—uncircumscribable by any social-historical context. Literature emerges, in all its historicity, from this break in social-historical context. The intelligibility of a text long after the death of the author and in vastly different historical contexts cannot be explained in historicist terms any more than it can be explained as the author's transcendence of death in an immortal work. This intelligibility enters the text through the door of the author's death. (The speech of immortals is unintelligible to us.) And this door, this opening to the out-of-context in any context, is always open. The end really can come at any time. Any meaningful story of the "death of the author"—another gruesome cliché of graveyard wisdom—is a story of the strange experience, through literature, of this opening *in life*.

The Writing of Our Dreams

The unobservable experience of the dream is the most common experience of this opening in life. The night of sleep can be observed and timed and placed in social and historical context. We make history in sleeping. But the "other night" of the dream cannot be observed and timed and placed in social and historical context. It's always "the other night"—almost a "once upon a time"—of the beginning of another kind of story. Dreams are not events in history, and though the tales of exceptional dreams—like those of kings—sometimes make it into recorded history, as a rule dreams enter the record in the lost column. Literature has a hand—the hand that holds a pen that leaves objective traces—in history. But even the least dreamy text has at least one foot in the "other night" of the dream at any given historical moment—one foot in the doorway leading both in and out of context that, in every given historical context, is the architectural expression of the structural possibility of the death of the author.

When it comes to the empirically determinable ink marks of writing, the common ground from which literary works spring can be socially and historically mapped and treated as a cultural site, to be tilled to this or that cultural purpose. But when it comes to the grayer areas of writing—the ambiguous kind of place in which Gray buries himself at the end of his *Elegy*—common ground is harder to map and harder yet to till.[17] This can make the grayer writers seem aloof and elitist, and it can lead elitist writers to seek the common ground of literature not in country churchyards but in the deathless society of a pantheon of great writers. Each of the writers studied in this book points, each in his own oblique way, to another, grayer kind of literary common ground—a ground neither historical nor transcendental. Blanchot, by far the most artless of these writers, gives out place-names as he points: "the other night," "the heart of the night." In the time and place that Blanchot names "the heart of the night," everybody has, every night, an intimate experience of the gray area of writing.

Though none of the writers studied in this book claims—like the troubadour who sleeps in the saddle or like the Coleridge of *Kubla Khan*—that works of writing are produced in his sleep, each brings to the fore of his work the restlessness that persists even in the depths of sleep, and each experiences that restlessness as an indication of the inevitability of writing. You can choose not to make works of writing, but you cannot choose not to dream. A person's dreams do not constitute an oeuvre of any kind, but, according to Freud's claim at the beginning of chapter 6 of the *Interpretation of Dreams*—a claim echoed, variously, by the other writers studied in this book—they do constitute a kind of writing. No one can do this writing. We can't make dreams the way we can make poems (and, even if we could, we could never publish them, or give them to a friend, or even keep them for ourselves). This doesn't mean, however, that we can pin them on a higher power.

Between the kind of writing that a god might do and the black, earthly ink that Milton's secretaries committed to the page (committing Milton, for all time, to a certain set of words) lies the big gray area of writing. Here Milton himself is as mute and inglorious as any mute inglorious Milton could be. If the world is, in some sense, a text—if the world is legible at all—it's not because the world is like a divinely written book but rather because the gray area of writing is as wide as the world, or at least as wide as that swath of the world where, at any given moment, it is night. And night falls for Milton at the same time as it falls for everyone else in England. In "the heart of the night"—in dreams—we all experience the world as writing. The dream is not an escape from the world and worldly responsibilities. It is rather nightly evidence of the impossibility of escape, so long as one is alive—the impossibility of complete sleep. The writers studied in this book feel this impossibility strongly and feel it as an impossibility of escaping writing, even by not writing. The kind of writing that a writer does may, as the troubadour and Coleridge claim, continue in the depths of sleep, but, if it does, that's only one expression of the inescapable ongoing movement of the writing that can never get done, never take the publishable form of this or that objectively realized work—the writing of our dreams. In the depths of sleep, the world continues to come to us in the form of writing that not even a god could ever do.

This writing is impossible to escape precisely because it is impossible to do. This book is an exploration of the strange logic of this consequence, the ethics of this literary responsibility. Nowhere is this strange logic more systematically worked out than in Beckett, who finds a comedy in it that, though not exactly divine, cannot get old. Never has the impossibility of achieving the writing of our dreams been embraced so openly. This is not, however, a gesture of resignation. Though no one expresses the exhaustion left in the wake of the age of dreambooks better than he does, Beckett does not turn away from the dream in that exhaustion. On the contrary, in his embrace of the impossibility of achieving the writing of our dreams, Beckett clings to the dream with a new resolve, holding us near enough to it and steady enough before it to begin to read it in the way that the dreambooks of the first half of the twentieth century would have us read it—"to read what was never written."[18]

"It's all right," says Beckett's Moran, "I'm not going to tell you a dream properly so called."[19] Beckett only seldom tells a dream "properly so called," preferring the tale of the telling itself and of the losing of everything that telling involves. But leading us ever back to the dry well from which they spring, his tales of the telling itself and of the losing of everything lead us ever back to the heart of the sleepless night we spend in dreams. Moran begins his account of his restless search for the cause of his restlessness here: "It is midnight. The rain is beating on the windows" (92/125). The final lines of his account underline the fiction in these sentences:

> Then I went back into the house and wrote, It is midnight. The rain is beating on the windows. It was not midnight. It was not raining. (176/239)

As I'll show in chapter 3, this underlining of the fiction in these sentences doesn't falsify them. It wasn't another time of day that could have been named but wasn't, and the weather wasn't otherwise in any reportable way. Here at the end of his account, Moran has become another. In passing, he is spoken of in the third person in such a way that it is not entirely clear that he is still the first-person speaker of these final lines:

> I have spoken of a voice telling me things. I was getting to know it better now, to understand what it wanted. It did not use the words that Moran had been taught when he was little and that he in turn had taught his little one. (175–76/238)

We may be approaching something like Samuel Beckett here in this final first person. Whatever we may be approaching, the approach certainly brings us closer to a truth. But this truth is not of a kind that could ever be stated in the form of "it was really x time when I wrote this, and the weather was y." The truth is that it was neither. Whatever night it really was or wasn't, the night on which writing began—the night on which Beckett first became another, now named Molloy, now named Moran, then Malone, and so on right through *The Unnamable*—was always "the other night." If it weren't, the source of Beckett's fictions would be namable, and *The Unnamable* would be just smoke and mirrors.

In fact, the stakes are much higher in fiction as Beckett understands it. Everyone is caught up in the endless chain of speakers in which Beckett finds himself caught up in his fiction. "Here Comes Everybody," says Joyce in *Finnegans Wake,* without quite knowing what he's saying. In Beckett, what Joyce says actually comes true. It's not that everyone is somehow made present in Beckett's art—that, in Beckett's effacing of himself, "poetry is made by everyone" as Lautréamont wished. Rather, the endless chain by which one speaker is connected to the next in Beckett connects us all; so long as no namable subject can be placed at the end of it, we have to see ourselves as linked in it. This chain of speakers is not exactly a great chain of being. No being holds the end of it or stretches along it. It's not a medium of communication over which the presence of subjects can be extended such that they are made present to each other over vast distances of space and time. Beckett's endless chain of speakers binds us to each other in the depths of our absence to each other and not in spite of it. We are bound to each other, in the odd logic of Beckett's fictions, by our common absence at the origin of the words we speak to each other—bound to each other in our alienation from the words we speak. These words we speak are never all ours, and this, much more than any unspeakable presence or communion or romance of a human family, connects us.

Beckett's wandering speakers are barred from communion with any presence at the source of their words—with any final instance of the power to speak. This bar keeps them going, keeps them speaking, far beyond the limits of their powers of speech (going on, says the unnamable last speaker of Beckett's trilogy, is as impossible as stopping).[20] In their endless alienation from the words they speak, they speak for everyone, but not as any kind of elect or according to any familiar logic of indirect representation or of writing as a form of representation. Like him, Beckett's speakers are often writers, but they speak for everyone who doesn't write—for all those whom Gray had to represent as "mute and inglorious Miltons"—by writing without knowing how:

> How, in such conditions, can I write, to consider only the manual aspect of that bitter folly? I don't know. . . . It is I who write, who cannot raise my hand from my knee.[21]

This miraculous writing of latter-day mute inglorious Miltons is not magic. It's not the work of the slight of hand of a magician named Samuel Beckett. Of course it's Beckett who writes the trilogy. Beckett commits the trilogy to paper on nights and days that can be dated and noted and about which we can, through historical study, know the weather. But "to consider only the manual aspect of [the] bitter folly" of writing is to fail to consider the broader sense of writing that Beckett insists upon in writing of speakers who write without lifting their hands from their knees.

As is the case in all literature, everything said in Beckett is writing. Beckett's speakers wonder without end at how this can be. Their wonder would be grating and boring if Beckett and we didn't share in it—if "because Beckett wrote it" were any sort of satisfying answer to their questions. "Who's Beckett?" asks Beckett in every word that he writes. This sort of question is of the most general interest precisely because no one can answer it for anyone else. We're all equally alone in this line of questioning, alone with the words and names that we can't help but share. To remember that everyone dreams and everyone dreams alone is to remember, among other things, this. The relentless and relentlessly limiting identification of people in contemporary culture as x, y, or z depends upon a systematic forgetting that everyone dreams and dreams alone. In speaking of an interconnection beyond any determinable shared identity—an interconnection in the very alienation from words that keeps us speaking—Beckett's speakers don't save their dreams from "the sable chain and dumb enchantment" of which Keats speaks with such regret in *The Fall of Hyperion* (lines 10–11). They only rarely speak of dreams, "properly so called." But they save themselves from the more patronizing prickings of liberal pity like Keats's—"pity these have not / Traced upon vellum or wild Indian leaf / the shadows of melodious utterance" (lines 4–6)—by speaking with a new rigor of an experience of writing considered beyond its "manual aspect." Where Keats had to morbidly divide the writing hand—"this warm scribe my hand . . . in the grave" (line 18)—from the rest of the writer in order to gesture toward the writing of his dreams, Beckett's speakers speak of writing without hands or other means to write. Where lack of means had kept Keats's "savages" and "fanatics" from writing and the laurels that it brings—"bare of laurel they live, dream, and die" (line 7)—none of Beckett's speakers, not even those in the most extreme lack of means, can escape writing. All glamour of all laurels is lost in the bargain. What's gained is a bracing sense of the restlessness of the speaking, dreaming animal, a sense beyond pity and guilt of the sublimely agitating interconnection of absolutely everyone in the art of losing—the art of reading the writing of our dreams—that is literature.

ONE

The Dream as Writing: Freud's Theory

The Problem of the Experience of the Dream

Some dreams, like the dreams of prophets, may be dreamt to be told to others, but only the dreamer can perceive his or her dream. This defining characteristic of the experience of a dream has been cited both to dismiss dreams as meaningless and to grant them special authority. Freud's first thesis in the *Interpretation of Dreams* is that dreams are meaningful and capable of being interpreted. But he argues that they are not meaningful considered as perceptual experiences. Rather, Freud finds that the meaning of a dream can be approached only if the dream is treated as what the dreamer can tell of it to another person and not as the perceptual experience that precedes and often seems to flee telling. For the purposes of interpretation, "Whatever the dreamer tells us must count as his dream, without regard to what he may have forgotten or altered in recalling it."[1]

According to Freud, the first barrier to the interpretation of a dream is the dreamer's attachment to the perceptual experience as such. Freud thus "asks the dreamer . . . to free himself from the impression of the manifest dream, to divert his attention from the dream as a whole onto the separate portions of its content and to report . . . in succession everything that occurs to him in relation to each of these portions—what associations present themselves to him if he focuses on each of them separately."[2] No dream can be interpreted psychoanalytically without following out the dreamer's associations on the elements of the dream, and Freud is only irritated when André Breton and others mail well-woven dreams to him for interpretation without pulling them apart and offering associations on their strands.

Freudian loosening of attachment to the enthralling perceptual experience of the dream lowers the dreamer's anxiety about whether what he or she is telling is faithful and true to what he or she has seen in the dream. Fidelity to the perceptual experience as such often dictates a mournful tone in the telling of a dream. A rich and profound experience has left a bittersweet taste on the tip of the dreamer's tongue. The experience is represented in words as lying beyond words. Freud is sensitive to this pathos on which so much of the beauty of dream-tales depends. But the pathos points, in his account, to anxiety about the meaning of dreams. It functions as a barrier to interpretation, and this barrier has to be lowered. This is a risky operation, however, as psychoanalysis loses its edge if it dissolves the barrier completely. The interpretation of dreams becomes a cozy and circular science when, in emphasizing the told at the expense of the seen, it gets chatty and forgets entirely the feeling that something really was seen—when it forgets entirely the feeling that one is alone with one's dream.

Freud manages to retain a bracing sense of the experience of the dream by radically reframing it. According to Freud's theory, what had seemed to be a perceptual experience of images of things can be shown, on interpretation, to have been an experience of writing. Freud's discovery of the meaning of dreams begins in the discovery that there is language there—that what seem to be images of things are in fact images of words, characters of a kind of pictographic writing. Seen as images of things, the dream dazzles but doesn't yield its sense. Its sense lies in the words it represents. Once the attachment to the dream as a perceptual experience is loosened, another, subtler sense of the experience emerges. The dream turns out to have been an experience of language, which cannot be understood as an object of perception. To find, upon waking, the words that the dream delivers is to begin to remember an experience that we cannot fail to miss so long as we're having it.

Nothing is easier to forget than this necessarily missed experience, and it is easy to miss Freud's attachment to it in all of his severe talk of the need to sever attachments to the dream as a perceptual experience. In his zeal to lower anxiety about the meaning of dreams enough so that his readers and his patients will admit it, Freud doesn't fully articulate the anxiety that must remain if psychoanalysis is to remain on its toes. But an anxiety lingers behind everything that he says about seeing the dream as writing—the anxiety characteristic of the experience of writing. When Freud's account of the meaningfulness of dreams ceases to seem outrageous and dream-messages begin to become decipherable in the way that he describes, the outrageousness of the proposition on which that account rests comes into full view. It may work to call these images that we see in our sleep "writing," but the more we say it, the stranger it sounds. According to Freud's theory, the dream unfolds on condition that it isn't seen as writing while it is unfolding. So if the theory is right, we would cease to dream the moment we became truly comfortable with the idea that what we're really faced with in our dreams is writing—comfortable enough to hold onto it in our sleep. Freud's theory of dreams rests on a proposition that, if true, cannot be comfortably accepted. We cannot fully face the writing of our dreams. The aim of this chapter is to articulate something of the writing anxiety implied in Freud's vision of the dream as writing.

Seeing the Dream as Writing

According to Freud, the images that we perceive in a dream are the result of a process of "regression" from ideation to perception, in which "thoughts are transformed into images, mainly of a visual sort; that is to say, word-presentations are taken back to the thing-presentations which correspond to them."[3] What Freud calls the "latent content" of the dream consists of "word-presentations."[4] The "dream-work" transforms these word-presentations into the images that we perceive in the dream—the "manifest content" of the dream. It can't be denied that these images represent things. But, seen as a representation of things, the dream doesn't make sense. In order to make sense of the dream, the interpreter has to look at the dream not in terms of its "pictorial value" (*Bilderwert*) but as a "picture-puzzle" (*Bilderrätsel*), the solution of which is a linguistic expression.[5] Famously, Freud likens the dream to a rebus:

> Suppose I have a picture-puzzle, a rebus, in front of me. It depicts a house with a boat on its roof, a single letter of the alphabet, the figure of a running man whose head has been conjured away, and so on. Now I might be misled into raising objections and declaring that the picture as a whole and its component parts are nonsensical. A boat has no business to be on the roof of a house, and a headless man cannot run. Moreover, the man is bigger than the house; and if the whole picture is intended to represent a landscape, letters of the alphabet are out of place in it since such objects do not occur in nature. But obviously we can only form a proper judgment of the rebus if we put aside criticisms such as these of the whole composition and its parts and if, instead, we try to replace each separate element by a syllable or word that can be represented by that element in one way or other. The words which are put together in this way are no longer nonsensical but may form a poetical phrase of the greatest beauty and significance. A dream is a picture-puzzle of this sort and our predecessors in the field of dream-interpretation have made the mistake of treating the rebus as a pictorial composition: and as such it has seemed to them nonsensical and worthless.[6]

According to Freud, though it may seem that we are seeing things, what we are really seeing in dreams is a "pictographic script" (*Bilderschrift*)—a form of writing.[7]

"Writing" is not an easy word to define, as it can be used in radically different senses. An electrocardiogram may be a kind of writing, but it's a far cry from Linear B. Without defining the word in a way that would account for all of its different uses, we can say that the word "writing" is the common name for that kind of image that serves primarily to represent words. Writing may, as in a dream, represent things secondarily (that is, it may represent words by means of the representation of things), other kinds of images may represent words secondarily, and the differences (1) between words and things and (2) between primary and secondary representation are by no means stable and clear. But when we take an image to be aiming, in the final analysis, at a representation of linguistic material, then we are taking it to be writing. It's at least in this broad and common sense of the word that the images we see in dreams must be considered a form of writing, if Freud is right about what those images represent.

The discovery that the dream is a form of writing begins in an inkling that the dream is not what it seems. The first step in the Freudian interpretation of a dream is to distinguish between the manifest content of the dream and its latent content. In its first instance, the distinction takes the form of an opposition between appearances and reality. The dream appears to be a representation of things, but it is really a representation of words. The Freudian interpretation of dreams begins in the sense that what we perceive in dreams is "a deception, a *façade*,"[8] behind which lies something else. Though the discovery that the dream is a form of writing begins in this sense, the discovery complicates the opposition of appearances and reality on which it depends. We don't know on which side of the opposition to place writing. On the one hand, writing is what the manifest content of the dream really is, despite appearances. The manifest content of the dream is writing, though it appears to be another kind of representation. Seeing that the dream is writing is, in this sense, seeing through false appearances. However, to see this is to see that the dream has latent content beyond appearances. And the writing of the dream is its manifest content seen as a representation of this realm beyond appearances. Though the dream may really be writing, this writing remains on the side of the manifest content of the dream and is not part of the "reality"—the latent content—that it represents.

Appearances would be saved best if the story of the discovery that the manifest content of the dream is a form of writing were told as a story of one kind of appearance (illusion, false appearance) giving way to another (abstract representation). As a second kind of appearance, the dream as writing could be distinguished from the dream as façade while remaining within the realm of appearances. But such a story would have to suppress the thorough inter-implication of the two kinds of appearance. It is essential to the dream's mode of abstract representation that it produce a figural façade to cover up its own abstraction. It is essential to the form of writing encountered in dreams that it be puzzling. The writing of the dream is a picture-puzzle—a kind of writing the aim of which is to hide meaning as much as it is to disclose it. It is perfectly in line with the basic purpose of this writing that the dream appear, at first glance, to be the farthest thing in the world from writing. So, if the dream is indeed the puzzling kind of writing that Freud says it is, then its initial appearance not to be has to be considered an effect of this writing and not an appearance of a completely different order. The figural concealment of itself as abstract representation of words is part of the puzzling way in which this writing represents words.

Because the puzzling writing of the dream *presents itself* as a perceptual experience of things, the psychoanalytical breaking of the attachment to this hallucinatory experience of things in order to get at the words that are really there is the breaking of a spell cast in writing, and not on it or over it. The hallucinatory experience of things in the dream is already an experience of writing. This complicates Freud's demand that the dreamer "free himself from the impression of the manifest dream." To free oneself from the spell of the hallucinatory show is to see that the dream was always writing, but it's in the nature of the writing it always was to hide itself in the guise of a perceptual experience. We see the writing of our dreams not through this guise but in it. To see it undisguised would be to lose sight of it. So the breaking of the spell of the hallucinatory experience is a delicate affair. For the dream to be legible, some sense of the nocturnal brilliance of the disguise must hold. What memory of this brilliance can survive the breaking of the spell of the hallucinatory perceptual experience? What sense can we retain of the nocturnal experience of the dream as writing?

Deconstruction and the Dream as Writing

Freud provokes these questions in claiming that the dream is a form of writing, but he never confronts them directly. He needs to conceive of the dream as a form of writing in order to describe how it is that it represents words, but he leaves the conception quite loose. In this way, he avoids the worst of the metaphysical cramping that sets in when one tries to find a fixed location for the writing of the dream within the opposition of appearances and reality by means of which it is first brought to light. Moments like the opening of chapter 6 of the dreambook, in which he openly calls the dream a form of writing, are rare. More often he works by analogy. The dream is *like* hieroglyphics, or *like* pictographic writing. However, as in his remarks on "The Philological Interest of Psychoanalysis," Freud presents the analogy as "complete":

> If we reflect that the means of representation in dreams are principally visual images and not words, we shall see that it is even more appropriate to compare dreams with a system of writing than with language. In fact the interpretation of dreams is completely analogous [*durchaus analog*] to the decipherment of an ancient pictographic script such as Egyptian hieroglyphics.[9]

What difference there is between a relation of complete analogy and an identity is subtle, but speaking in terms of analogy, however complete, permits Freud a looseness that speaking in terms of identity wouldn't allow for. For Freud, the important thing is to present a surprising and illuminating likeness and to see what can be seen in that new light. And the most important thing that can be seen in that light is the "royal road to a knowledge of the unconscious activities of the mind" unfolding before him.[10] The destination of this road is the properly psychoanalytical interest of psychoanalysis, which Freud pursues tirelessly. But along the way he says that the "complete analogy" between dreams and pictographic writing systems is the central "philological interest of psychoanalysis," which he considers to have been insufficiently pursued:

> If this conception of the method of representation in dreams [the conception of dreams as "completely analogous" to pictographic writing] has not yet been followed up, this, as will be readily understood, must be ascribed to the fact that psycho-analysts are entirely ignorant of the attitude and knowledge with which a philologist would approach such a problem as that presented by dreams.[11]

The thinker who has pursued this "philological interest of psychoanalysis" furthest is Jacques Derrida, who picks up on Freud's articulation of it in his essay on "Freud and the Scene of Writing":

> It is with a graphematics still to come, rather than with a linguistics dominated by an ancient phonologism, that psychoanalysis sees itself as destined to collaborate. Freud recommends this *literally* in a text from 1913, and in this case we have nothing to add, interpret, alter . . . "It seems more appropriate to compare dreams with a system of writing than with language."[12]

In his embrace of the analogy that Freud draws between dreams and writing, Derrida underlines the difference on which the sense of any analogy—and especially such a "complete analogy"—depends. For Derrida, Freud's vision of the dream as writing opens up a new way of thinking about the difference between writing that we read in the world (the coded inscriptions that present themselves to the bodily senses) and writing in an extramundane sense (traditionally conceived of as "divine writing," or the universal writing of truth in the soul, to be read, if at all, only with the mind's eye). Traditionally, the former is understood by paradoxical turns as both the figural representation of the latter, which is more original, and as the proper meaning of "writing"—what one is properly talking about when one talks about "writing." Deconstructive consideration of the question of writing registers the seeming contradiction in this state of affairs without trying to dissolve it by pursuing further inversions of the oppositions (original writing versus secondary writing; proper meaning versus figural meaning) according to the same chiastic structure: "It is not, therefore, a matter of inverting the literal meaning and figurative meaning but of determining the 'literal' meaning of writing as metaphoricity itself," or *différance*.[13] In "Freud and the Scene of Writing," Derrida argues that Freud's conception of the workings of writing in the dream "prefigures the meaning of writing in general."[14]

"Writing in general" or "general writing" or "writing *avant la lettre*" is neither the a priori concept of writing nor an object of sense experience, in any ordinary conception of sense experience. It is rather what Rodolphe Gasché calls a "quasitranscendental synthesis."[15] According to Derrida, Freud's conception of the dream as a form of writing makes a counterintuitive concept like "writing *avant la lettre*" thinkable by making problematic all of the basic oppositions (such as the opposition between empirical and ideal) by which the concept of writing has traditionally been determined. Central among these is the opposition between images and words. Freud shows that the dream represents words the way writing, in the mundane sense of the word, represents words. But to show that there are words there where they don't seem to be is to show as well that writing—the image of words—is not what it has traditionally seemed to be. It is not simply a means of extending speech beyond earshot. On Derrida's view, "Freud doubtless conceives of the dream as a displacement similar to an original form of writing which puts words on stage without becoming subservient to them; and he is thinking here, no doubt, of a model of writing irreducible to speech."[16]

According to the traditional model, writing is a vehicle of speech. It extends speech beyond the spatial reach the author's voice and, potentially, beyond the temporal limit of his or her life. Communicating the author's speech to the reader, it connects presence to faraway presence. Whether this connection is celebrated for its strength or cursed for its weakness, writing is seen as an artificial means of extending the presence of a speaker over a gap. According to the alternative model of writing that Derrida finds prefigured in Freud, writing is, from the start, independent of the presence of a subject who might speak for it. In any definition of writing, writing is defined by its legibility in the absence of the subject who might speak for it. Derrida argues that this legibility can be properly explained only when writing's original freedom from its originating subject is fully recognized. However, this freedom practically implies its own repression, as it entails an extension of the domain of writing far beyond the limits set for it in ordinary language. The free space of "writing in general" is not this or that recognizable region. Rather, it covers the whole realm of possible experience:

> This structural possibility of being severed from its referent or signified (and therefore from communication and its context) seems to me to make of every mark, even if oral, a grapheme in general, that is, as we have seen, the nonpresent *remaining* of a differential mark cut off from its alleged "production" or origin. And I will extend this law even to all "experience" in general, if it is granted that there is no experience of *pure* presence, but only of chains of differential marks.[17]

Whether it is felt as a contortion of sense or a mind-opening reach, such an extreme stretching of the concept of writing can occur only in a dreamy dimension. It would not be thinkable without the example of the dream as it appears in Freud's theory. Everybody, literate or not, dreams. So if the dream is as Freud says it is—a form of writing—then everyone is intimately and unavoidably involved in writing, whether or not they read or write in the ordinary senses of those verbs. The dream is not "writing in general," but it is a form of writing in which the limits of ordinary form are removed in such a way that something like "writing in general" begins to become distinguishable (both from writing in the mundane sense and from divine writing, or the universal psychography of truth). The outlines of the possibility of such a concept as "writing in general"—an unlimited writing at work wherever there is experience and not only in this or that work of writing—begin to appear when the dream, the most common experience in the world, is seen as a form of writing.

If the dream is a form of writing, then, unlike an alphabet or a system of hieroglyphics, it is unlimited not only in its "use"—everybody, literate or not in this or that writing system, dreams—but also in its elements. Though Freud does allow for a handful of standardized symbols in dreams, these do not function as a set of elements. Anything under the sun can become a character in the writing of dreams, and many an oneiric wonder is born of this. What system there is to this writing comes down to a set of basic operations by which the linguistic expressions that the writing represents are converted into written form. (Freud describes the way these operations work at length in chapter 6 of *The Interpretation of Dreams.*) But the same linguistic expression could, passing through these same operations, be represented in 1001 different ways. If this weren't the case, dreams would not be nearly as puzzling as they are. The writing of the dream is particularly puzzling because, though it can be deciphered, one can never become literate in it the way one can become literate in an ordinary writing system. The logic of the basic operations can be learned, but there's no learning a set of elements, as the set is not closed. If we could learn this writing the way we can learn an alphabet or the way an ancient Egyptian scribe could learn hieroglyphics, then we could make our own dreams. But, whether or not advocates of "lucid dreaming" are right in claiming that we can control our dreams to some extent, we cannot make our dreams the way we can make a poem. It may be possible, as Coleridge claims in his prefatory note to *Kubla Khan,* to write poems in dreams, but it's not possible to make a dream in anything like the way we can make a poem upon waking.

If the dream were the limited kind of writing we could learn to do, then we could also remember dreams better than we do. One of the most remarkable things about our dreams is how easily we forget the great majority of them. Though the writing we do in waking life can be ephemeral—texts can be burnt or otherwise lost—no writing that we do on paper or even on screen could be as fleeting as the average dream. One can, upon waking, commit a dream to the sort of writing that can be preserved in a folder or a file, but the writing of the dream can't be stored. Much of the pathos surrounding dreaming comes down to this certainty of loss. What's lost is often felt particularly acutely when one tries to tell a dream. A common conceptualization of this feeling has it that the dream is an experience beyond the reach of human language. (The experience can be praised or dismissed equally well in these terms.) The sense of an experience lost to human language is only made more acute when one tries to write down a dream. This can leave the writer of his or her dreams with the feeling that the dream is the farthest thing in the world from writing, or so close but yet so far.

Fighting this feeling, Freud insists upon a coldness to the habitual pathos of the lost experience. But his vision of the dream as writing implies a new pathos of the loss. When writing can no longer be considered to be in its essence (which is to say, in every possible instance) a specialized technique, then it can no longer be kept out of the hair of experience in general. Freud's discovery of writing in the dream implies a radical and general entanglement of writing and experience. Deconstruction can be seen as the conceptual explication of this entanglement. In this general entanglement, we find ourselves tied to our lost experiences in new ways. The loss of a dream becomes both deeper and less upsetting when what we begin to forget upon waking is thought of not as an experience of presence to marvelous things but as an experience of not being there—an experience of the absence in the heart of writing. Freud's description of the way that jokes occur to us in our absence holds as well for dreams, except that in dreams the absence is night-long:

> Jokes possess yet another characteristic which fits satisfactorily into the view of the joke-work which we have derived from dreams. We speak, it is true, of "making" a joke; but we are aware that when we do so our behavior is different from what it is when we make a judgment or make an objection. A joke has quite outstandingly the characteristic of being a notion that has occurred to us "involuntarily." What happens is not that we know a moment beforehand what joke we are going to make, and that all it then needs is to be clothed in words. We have an indefinable feeling, rather, which I can best compare with an "*absence*" [*Absenz*], a sudden release of intellectual tension, and then all at once the joke is there—as a rule ready-clothed in words.[18]

Experience Without Presence: The Dream-Work

The dreamer is no more present while dreaming than the things he or she sees in the dream are present. This is a crucial difference between a hallucination in waking life and a dream. The subject of a waking hallucination can respond to questions about the experience he or she is having as he or she is having it, whereas the dreamer can respond only once the experience is over. This is not merely a loss of the power of speech, as the dreamer can no more respond by signs or gestures than he or she can respond in spoken words to questions posed to him or her from the world in which his or her body lies asleep. Absence to this world could and often has been conceived of as presence to another, perhaps truer, world. Certainly, the dreamer can seem to respond in the dream to questions posed to him or her from within the dreamworld. But the Freudian conception of the dream does not allow for any two-world view of things. According to Freud, no speech heard or said in dreams is uttered live. Any words and phrases appearing in dreams are hand-me-downs snipped from discourse uttered by day in the old, waking world:

> When anything in a dream has the character of direct speech, that is to say, when it is said or heard and not merely thought (and it is easy as a rule to make the distinction with certainty), then it is derived from something actually spoken in waking life—though, to be sure, this something is merely treated as raw material and may be cut up and slightly altered and, more especially, divorced from its context.[19]

> Where spoken sentences occur in dreams and are expressly distinguished as such from thoughts, it is an invariable rule that the words spoken in the dream are derived form spoken words remembered in the dream-material.[20]

> For the dream-work cannot actually *create* speeches. However much speeches and conversations, whether reasonable or unreasonable in themselves, may figure in dreams, analysis invariably proves that all that the dream has done is to extract from the dream-thoughts fragments of speeches which have really been made or heard.[21]

When words appear in the dream, their status is no different from that of the things that appear there:

> Words are treated in dreams as though they were concrete things, and for that reason they are apt to be combined in just the same way as presentations of concrete things.[22]

Any words heard or spoken in the dream are to be regarded simply as things among the other things perceived in the dream, and, for Freud, there is no other world in which the things perceived in the dream can be accurately thought of as present.

The dreamer can only dream that the words he or she says or hears in his or her dream are uttered live and in the present. The only thing like live speech in the dream is the elaboration of the dream-script. The things seen in dreams represent words, according to Freud, so it may make sense, within Freud's theory, to speak of these represented words as being present in the dream. But the dreamer cannot respond to these words in the present. It's only once the dream is over that the dream-script becomes recognizable as such and a response becomes possible.

If the dreamer could respond live to the words disguised as images that his or her dream addresses to him or her, sleep would not resemble death as closely as it does. The likeness of sleep to death, which has prompted at least one prince to seize his father's crown before his father's death, prompts the analytical philosopher Norman Malcolm to claim, in his important account of dreaming, that the dream can no more be considered a life experience than death can be considered a life experience. As Wittgenstein, Malcolm's teacher, puts it: "Death is not an event of life. Death is not lived through."[23] The moment of death, if such a thing could ever be pinned down, would be the moment at which the subject of life experiences becomes absent. "I am dead" cannot be pronounced without performative contradiction. For Malcolm, the analogy between sound sleep and death is such that the dream cannot even be considered a kind of seeming, as there is no subject present in sound sleep to whom anything might seem: "to a person who is sound asleep, 'dead to the world,' things cannot even seem."[24] The only phenomenon one can speak of in dreaming is the phenomenon of telling the dream upon waking:

> It is this peculiar phenomenon of speaking in the past tense after sleep, the phenomenon called "telling a dream," that provides the sense of the proposition that dreams occur during sleep.[25]

As a result, whatever the dreamer tells and only what the dreamer tells counts as the dream, supposing that he or she tells it in good faith:

> If after sleep a person relates that he thought and did and experienced such-and-such (all of this being false), and if he is not lying, pretending, or

> inventing, then we say "he dreamt it." "That is the language-game!" That he really had a dream and that he is under the impression that he had a dream: these are the same thing . . . In the case of remembering a dream there is no contrast between correctly remembering and seeming to oneself to remember—here they are identical! (It can even appear surprising that we should speak of "remembering" a dream.)[26]

What experience there is of the dream is an experience of having dreamt. There is no present tense experience of the dream against which to measure the truth or falsehood of one's past tense accounts. It often occurs to us to tell our dreams, but "a dream is *not* an occurrence."[27]

Though this conclusion goes against every intuitive understanding of dreaming, we are obliged to accept it so long as we accept (1) that dreaming cannot be understood as a kind of presence to anything and (2) that there is no possibility of experience without presence. We've seen that Freud's account implies the first of these propositions, and that he is thus unsentimental when it comes to the experience of the dream: "Whatever the dreamer tells us must count as his dream, without regard to what he may have forgotten or altered in telling it." But despite his attitude of suspicion about the experience, Freud doesn't go so far as to suggest that the dream is not an occurrence in sleep and that there is no experience of the dream during sleep. This means that Freud's theory must allow for the possibility of a kind of experience without presence. Freud doesn't speak of "experience" in this strange sense, but his account of the dream-work is an account of what is really going on in dreams as they occur in sleep. Freud suggests that the impression that one has forgotten more of a dream than one can remember is really a disguised memory, not of this or that content, but of the night-long process of the dream-work itself:

> The feeling of having dreamt a great deal during the night and of only having retained a little of it may in fact have some other meaning, such as that the dream-work has been perceptibly proceeding all through the night but has only left a short dream behind. It is no doubt true that we forget dreams more and more as time passes after waking; we often forget them in spite of the most painstaking efforts to recall them. But I am of the opinion that the extent of this forgetting is as a rule overestimated.[28]

"The impression that we have dreamt a great deal more than we can reproduce is very often based on an illusion" in which the manifest content of the dream and the dream-work are confused.[29] If there is an experience of the dream as event, it is an experience not of this or that content of the dream but of the working of the dream-work itself.

In Freud's theory, the perceptual experience of the dream turns out to be a ruse, but this does not imply that the dream is, as Malcolm would have it, truly what one says about it and only what one says about it when one is speaking truthfully. Looking at what is said and only at what is said rather than staring into the abyss of the fleeting experience makes it possible to discover a latent content that can be articulated. Both the manifest content of the dream and the latent content of the dream are expressible in language. Freud sometimes talks about articulation of the latent content as the "practical task" of psychoanalytical dream interpretation.[30] However, he does not consider articulation of the latent content to be articulation of the truth of the dream. The dream is truly neither this content nor that content. Rather, the dream is, in its essence, the dream-work by which the one sort of content is transformed into the other.

Throughout his later writings on dreams, Freud insists that the dream should not be confused with its latent content any more than it should be confused with its manifest content. See, for example, the famous footnote added to the *Interpretation of Dreams* in 1925:

> But now that analysts at least have become reconciled to replacing the manifest dream by the meaning revealed by its interpretation, many of them have become guilty of falling into another confusion which they cling to with equal obstinacy. They seek to find the essence of dreams in their latent content and in so doing they overlook the distinction between the latent dream-thoughts and the dream-work. At bottom, dreams are nothing other than a particular *form* of thinking, made possible by the conditions of the state of sleep. It is the *dream-work* which creates the form, and it alone is the essence of dreaming—the explanation of its particular nature.[31]

The dream-work cannot be seen without the articulation of the latent content of the dream, but the latent content is not the essence of the dream. By the same token, the unconscious wish that the dream expresses is not the essence of the dream. The unconscious wish is the force that drives (*Triebkraft*) the dream-work. There could be no dream without it, and the goal of "practical analysis" is to articulate it. But the dream is not reducible to the unconscious wish upon which it depends. Thus Freud's irritation at reductions of his theory to the punchline that a dream always represents the fulfillment of a wish:

> I could assume that . . . the "dream-work" was already familiar to my readers. But it will probably be wiser not to make that assumption. I have an impression that my *Interpretation of Dreams*, published in 1900, provoked more "bewilderment" than "enlightenment" among my fellow-specialists; and I know that wider circles of readers have been content to reduce the contents of the book to a catch-word ("wish-fulfillment") which can be easily remembered and conveniently misused.[32]

The unconscious wish powers the dream, which always expresses both that driving wish and the preconscious wish to sleep, along with many preconscious thoughts. The dream-work expresses, by compromise formations, the wishes of both of these agencies, but neither of these agencies can be considered agents of the dream-work. Though the subject of unconscious wishes can be discovered through analysis of the product of the dream-work (the subject of preconscious thoughts and wishes can be discovered upon ordinary, non-psychoanalytic self-reflection),[33] the subject of the unconscious is not a worker—it does not do the dream-work in which it invests its interests. According to Freud's theoretical *mise en scène* of the nightly production of dreams, the role of the unconscious is that of a capitalist who may or may not be his own entrepreneur but who certainly is not his own laborer:

> The position may be explained by an analogy. A daytime thought may very well play the part of *entrepreneur* for a dream; but the *entrepreneur*, who, as people say, has the idea and the initiative to carry it out, can do nothing without capital; he needs a *capitalist* who can afford the outlay, and the capitalist who provides the psychical outlay for the dream is invariably and indisputably, whatever may be the thoughts of the previous day, *a wish from the unconscious.*
>
> Sometimes the capitalist is himself the *entrepreneur.*[34]

Whether the entrepreneur in a particular dream is an unconscious wish or a preconscious thought has no effect on the basic workings of the dream:

> It is possible to distinguish between dreams *from above* and dreams *from below.* Dreams from below are those which are provoked by the strength of an

> unconscious (repressed) wish which has found a means of being represented in some of the day's residues. They may be regarded as inroads of the repressed into waking life. Dreams from above correspond to thoughts or intentions of the day before which have contrived during the night to obtain reinforcement from repressed material that is debarred from the ego . . . This distinction calls for no modification in the theory of dreams.[35]

The dream-work cannot be affected by the interests it expresses. This doesn't mean that the dream-work is freely done. A dream is always the servant of two masters, and the initial order for a dream must come from one or the other of these masters. But the origin of the order has no effect on the production process. The process itself is changeless, unthinking and unfeeling. "It does not think, calculate, or judge in any way at all; it restricts itself to giving things a new form":[36]

> There is no necessity to assume that any peculiar symbolizing activity of the mind is operating in the dream-work . . . [rather] dreams make use of any symbolizations which are already present in unconscious thinking.[37]

And the dream-work can no more conceive a feeling than it can forge its own thought. Any affect with which it works is ready-made. This is true even in cases of reversal of affect, where the dream-work might be supposed to produce the affect opposite to the one it finds in the content on which it is working: "Nor is it necessary to assume, in such cases either, that the dream-work *creates* contrary affects of this kind out of nothing; it finds them as a rule lying ready to hand in the material of the dream-thoughts."[38] Innocent of thought or feeling or of any interest to which a subject might incline, the dream-work cannot be altered by the initiative of any subjective agency, unconscious or preconscious. If it could, then it could be affected by what is said about dreams in psychoanalysis, where the negotiation between agencies is endless. According to Freud, both the manifest content and the latent content of dreams can be affected by the analytic treatment (and by other forms of suggestion, like telepathy), but he is adamant that the dream-work itself cannot be affected:

> On the mechanism of the dream-formation itself, on the dream-work in the strict sense of the word, one never exercises any influence: of that one may be quite sure.[39]

The validity of Freud's theory depends upon this indifference to influence in the heart of the dream. The manifest content and the latent content of a dream can be affected by interpretation, but the logic of the transformation of the one into the other cannot be a matter of interpretation if it is to give interpretation its rules. Freud agrees with Malcolm that there is no criterion for establishing whether or not an account of a dream is true vis à vis an experience. He therefore suspends the question of whether or not a patient's narrative of his or her dream is accurate. But, unlike Malcolm, he does not claim that there is no way of establishing that something independent of the waking experience of telling a dream is really going on in sleep. The dream-work is discovered through analysis of the telling of a dream, but it is independent of the subjective determinations everywhere at work in the telling and in the analysis. This doesn't mean that the dream-work is somehow objective. The truth of Freudian dream interpretation is neither subjective nor objective. No criterion of accuracy is applicable. The dream is not an experience of the kind on which one might accurately report. However, one can misrepresent a dream by representing it as the objectively realized work of a subject.

An Unfilled Opening: The Position of the Worker in the Dream-Work

Freud goes out of his way to avoid any characterization of a dream-worker in his theory of the dream-work. He gives us capitalist and entrepreneur but no figure of a laborer. This could be dismissed as a bourgeois repression of the fundamental role of labor in all production if Freud ever gave the capitalist or the entrepreneur credit for the dream-work and if the theory of the dream-work were not such a vivid account of a kind of work that no subject could possibly do. Though Freud's discovery of the unconscious via the interpretation of dreams is often taken to be the discovery that dreams are made by the unconscious, what Freud actually says is that we can read the investments of capital in the production of the manifest content of the dream out of the latent content, but that the dream-work—the work of making the dream—remains indifferent, in its essence, to the interests invested in it. A new dimension of the subject is discovered beyond consciousness. The unconscious can be an agent—it can "act out" of me: "what I am disavowing not only 'is' in me but sometimes 'acts' from out of me as well."[40] But the unconscious is not the agent responsible for the doing of the dream-work. Assuming responsibility for the agency of the unconscious that dreams reveal is not assuming responsibility for the making of the dream. The responsibility that psychoanalysis would have us assume for our dreams is of a different kind.

While the law and traditional morality have trouble determining responsibility for acts that are not consciously intended, psychoanalysis holds me responsible for the acting out of the unconscious in me—or rather shows me that this responsibility cannot be evaded:

> If I were to give way to my moral pride and tried to decree that for purposes of moral valuation I might disregard the evil in the id and need not make my ego responsible for it, what use would that be to me? Experience shows me that I nevertheless *do* take that responsibility, that I am somehow compelled to do so. Psycho-analysis has made us familiar with a pathological condition, obsessional neurosis, in which the poor ego feels itself responsible for all sorts of evil impulses of which it knows nothing, impulses which are brought up against it in consciousness but which it is unable to acknowledge. Something of this is present in every normal person.[41]

Dreams, like the symptoms of obsessional neurosis, are formations in which responsibility for unconscious acts and wishes is taken, whether one likes it or not. The dream is one of many ways in which responsibility for the unconscious is taken, but the unconscious is not responsible for doing the dream-work of making the dream. Responsibility for the unconscious is responsibility for the *content* of our dreams:

> Must one assume responsibility for the content of one's dreams? . . . Obviously one must hold oneself responsible for the evil impulses of one's dreams. What else is one to do with them? Unless the content of the dream (rightly understood) is inspired by alien spirits, it is part of my own being.[42]

Freud accepts no mythical projections of the content of dreams onto alien spirits. Insofar as the better part of us is unconscious, we are the stuff of dreams. This stuff, including the energy that the unconscious invests in the making of dreams, is ours. However, we can no more make our dreams than a god can make them for us.

Though the subject of the unconscious can be discovered in it, Freud does not attribute the work of making the dream to any subject that might stand behind it—not even to such a slippery subject as the subject of the unconscious. The dream is mine, but it is not made by me or by the other in me. The closest thing in Freud to a figure for the worker responsible for the doing of the dream-work is the figure of the dream itself as the "guardian of sleep." Though no laborer is to be found behind the dream-work, Freud characterizes the dream itself as a kind of laborer—a not exactly productive kind of night laborer. He introduces this figure in chapter 5 of *The Interpretation of Dreams*:

> All dreams are in a sense dreams of convenience: they serve the purpose of prolonging sleep instead of waking up. *Dreams are the* GUARDIANS *of sleep and not its disturbers.*[43]

The last appearance of the figure, from a text of 1938, slightly modifies the first:

> We shall be taking every experience into account if we say that a dream is invariably an *attempt* to get rid of a disturbance of sleep by means of a wish-fulfillment, so that the dream is a guardian of sleep. The attempt may succeed more or less completely; it may also fail, and in that case the sleeper wakes up, apparently woken precisely by the dream. So, too, there are occasions when that excellent fellow the night-watchman, whose business it is to guard the little township's sleep, has no alternative but to sound the alarm and waken the sleeping townspeople.[44]

In this strange turn of figurative speech, the dream is presented as an attempt by the dream itself—as guardian—to maintain the sleep that is the condition of its own production. The production of the dream is the dream's production of itself; the dream-work is the work of the dream, and the dream is a dizzying *mise en abîme* of its own production. This *mise en abîme* can be anxiety-provoking. However, in the absence of any other figure of the subject of the dream-work, the figure of the dream as worker is not avoidable. If no dream-worker can be found behind the dream-work, then there's no avoiding the conclusion that the dream makes itself.

In the absence of a dream-worker standing outside the dream, there's no getting around the self-reflexivity of the dream-work. And this self-reflexivity can make the dream seem entirely disconnected from anything outside itself. However, in Freud's theory—the practical aim of which is to connect the dream to the rest of mental life—this self-reflexivity is not a closed structure. In describing the dream as the guardian of sleep, Freud sees the dream as guarding an opening to the world against the attempts of the subject to close the opening by closing in upon itself. In Freud's theory, the wish to sleep is the subject's wish for complete narcissistic closure upon itself. "The wish to sleep endeavors to draw in all the cathexes sent out by the ego and to establish an absolute narcissism," says Freud.[45] But, because such closure would mean death, and sleep is not death, sleep depends, paradoxically, upon the partial frustration of the wish to sleep. An entirely dreamless sleep would not be sleep at all, but death. The dream guards sleep by maintaining open connections to the world against the subject's wish to withdraw completely into itself.

When the subject attempts to close itself off entirely in sleep, the resistance of the unconscious to such closure is discovered without fail:

> The repressed portion of the system *Ucs.* does not comply with the wish to sleep that comes from the ego . . . it retains its cathexis in whole or in part . . . Thus we should picture the situation which leads to the formation of dreams as follows. The wish to sleep endeavors to draw in all the cathexes sent out by the ego and to establish an absolute narcissism. This can only partly succeed, for what is repressed in the system *Ucs.* does not obey the wish to sleep.[46]

And sometimes some resistance will come from preconscious material as well:

> The possibility . . . that some of the preconscious thoughts of the day may also prove resistant and retain a part of their cathexis . . . must be recognized as a second breach of narcissism.[47]

The unconscious never sleeps. If it did, there could be no dream. But the sleeplessness of the unconscious is not the sleeplessness of the guardian of sleep. The latter represents the former, giving it expression in order to contain it enough for sleep to go on. But this representation is not just a pale, secondary image of the sleeplessness of the primary process. The dream is not only a figure of waking. As the "guardian of sleep," it is also itself a waking figure. This figure takes the place of the subject when the subject is absent to the world, non-responsive in sleep. My dream wakes so that I can sleep. It maintains the thread of experience over the radical gap in experience—the interruption in presence to the world—that sleep represents. The unconscious contributes the sleep-resistant metals out of which this thread is woven, but the dream-work weaves the thread by weaving around itself reflexively, according to its own inviolable procedures. The thread does not represent a continuity of presence. Rather, it is the line by which communication with the world is kept open, even in the absence of the subject.

This line is not a pseudo-umbilical cord connecting the subject to the world. Rather, it is the tie to the world that begins in the impossibility of reestablishing the lost umbilical connection. One particularly famous figure that Freud gives to the knotting of this tie is that of the navel of the dream. Freud often describes the attempt at narcissistic withdrawal from the world in sleep as an attempt to return to an embryonic state.[48] Within the terms of this description, the navel would be a figure for the closing off of any possibility of that withdrawal and therefore for the opening up of the unplumbable relation to the world that the dream watches over in sleep. Freud introduces the figure of the navel of the dream in a footnote to his interpretation of his dream of Irma's injection, declaring: "There is at least one spot in every dream at which it is unplumbable—a navel, as it were, that is its point of contact with the unknown."[49] And he returns to it in the last chapter of the dreambook:

> There is often a passage in even the most thoroughly interpreted dream which has to be left obscure; this is because we become aware during the work of interpretation that at that point there is a tangle of dream-thoughts which cannot be unraveled and which moreover adds nothing to our knowledge of the content of the dream. This is the dream's navel, the spot where it reaches down into the unknown.[50]

This spot marks the "ex-" of the separation of the child from the mother. The dream, as guardian of sleep, guards this spot. In watching its navel—in the self-reflexivity of its work as watchman—my dream maintains the tie by which I am most fundamentally bound to the world.

The dream only appears to be the experience of objects by a subject. According to Freud's theory, though the dream may seem to be a perceptual experience, it is really a break in the flow of this kind of experience of things. The work of the dream is the maintenance, over this break, of the possibility of experience in general. The only true experience of the dream possible in Freud's theory is the experience not of this or that worldly or otherworldly object but of the maintenance-work of the tying off/opening up of its own navel. The odd experience of the dream-work is the experience of a relation to the world that precedes and exceeds the subject and on which the possibility of any experience of objects depends. To experience this ongoing relation is to feel the restlessness in the heart of sleep that makes the difference between sleep and death and assures the little rest that sleep does afford.

Having Dreams, Having and Not Having Words

In the most extreme separation from the world, Freud discovers an ongoing relation. In the heart of our deepest rest, he discovers the impossibility of complete rest. Dreams would have no meaning, according to Freud's theory, if they were not the products of a restlessness that comes with the condition of not being able to separate oneself completely from the restlessly turning world. The dream is meaningful because it is the work of a kind of writing that keeps me implicated in the ongoing world even in my most extreme absence to it. Seen only as a perceptual experience, the dream doesn't connect and its meaning can't be reliably articulated. I am alone in the perception of my dream—alone with visions of things that can't be shared. The dream seems either too meaningful for words or meaningless. When what seems to be a perceptual experience is understood as an effect of a writing that aims to disguise itself as such, I am still alone, but my sense of isolation shifts. No one else can share the experience of my dream, but the experience is no longer an experience of things that can't be shared. The odd experience of the dream-work is an experience of a restless, universal process by which words are disguised as images of things. The discovery of words in the images we see in dreams is the discovery of the impossibility of complete isolation at the bottom of the most complete isolation possible. We couldn't know this impossibility if our sleep were dreamless.

Freud's discovery that the images in the dream represent words thus casts a new light on the anxiety about meaning associated with the impossibility of sharing the perceptual experience of the dream. The anxiety that presents itself as a function of being completely cut off from others turns out to be a function of the impossibility of separating oneself completely. It has its roots in separation—separation from the mother. But the symbol of this separation—the navel—is, for Freud, an image of the impossibility of closing off the opening to the world in dreams. The denial of the meaningfulness of dreams is a denial of this impossibility and an attempt to put an end to the restlessness encountered in the heart of sleep. The end of this restlessness would be the end of a writing anxiety on which the defense of the borders of sleep, and thus of life itself, depends.

Though it assures what rest is possible in this life, the relation to the world that Freud discovers in the heart of dreams is an anxious one. The relation doesn't take the comforting form of a correspondence with other people or with myself as another person. The comforting self-relationship that Cato finds in solitude—"never is he less alone than when he is by himself"[51]—is not to be found in dreams. I'm no more with myself than anyone else is with me in the experience of my dream. Rather, I find myself in a strange relationship with words that are mine, insofar as my dream is mine, but that I could not have been the source of. Upon waking, I can reconstruct the words and phrases written in the dream-script, and I can say, in retrospect, that the desires that they express are mine. In this sense, the words my dream delivers to me are more intimately mine than any words I could consciously dream up. But my desire doesn't make its own language. It's a creature of second-hand words. If it could make its own language, then I could make my own dreams.

I can say this or that and be held responsible as a speaking subject for what I say. And psychoanalysis can show me that whenever I speak—and certainly whenever I speak about my dreams—I am bound to be saying much more about myself than I think I'm saying. But though they may articulate the meaning of my life, I am not the source of the words I speak—the words themselves. This is so utterly obvious that it can easily pass unremarked by day. In showing me words that I can't recognize as such and can't respond to during the showing, my dream shows me again, with a vividness that makes full memory of the lesson impossible, that my words precede me. I can make a poem or a speech, but I can't make the language I speak. My dream is the ageless child of this impotence that every child finds him or herself in when first confronted with language. A child usually learns sooner or later to speak, but no amount of language learning can place a speaker at the origin of language and end the alienation from words into which he or she enters at birth. All human experience begins and unfolds in this alienation. Here begins my life in words, the only life I have—a life I have only in the same tenuous sense in which I may be said to have words.

In the alienation from words that comes with a life in words, any claim of responsibility for one's desires is more likely to fall flat than not. It's likely that one's distance from one's desires will either be insufficiently represented, thus repressing any sense of the opening of the possibility of the experience of desire in the first place, or it will be overrepresented, thus effecting a disavowal of the desire itself. Freud's theory of dreams does not present us with any foolproof solution to this rhetorical bind. His own confessions are problematic to say the least. But Freud's theory shows us that the rhetorical bind is no more avoidable than our bond to the world is avoidable. Our dreams keep us in it even as they give expression to our deepest desires to be done with it. They keep us in it by holding us to words that are always not ours before they are ours. If our dreams deceive us, presenting us with words in the shape of alien things, it is because words couldn't continue to come to us at all if we could speak to ourselves directly, without any detour through figures of the outside world from which words come and to which they return. The distortion that we encounter in dreams is not just sugar to make the poison or the medicine of the unconscious go down. It's a function of the alienation from words that is the condition of the possibility of any experience of words. Writing must alter speech in giving an image of it, and, whether or not we know how to read and write in any mundane script, it's by the ceaseless movement of this alteration—by the dream-work—that words come and continue to come to us over the distance—call it the world—that separates us from them.

TWO

Dream and Writing in Blanchot

The Experience of Writing, "Impossibility," and the Dream

In his critical works, Blanchot often speaks of an "experience": *The Experience of Mallarmé* or *The Experience of* Igitur, *The Experience of Proust* and *The Experience of Lautréamont.*[1] This "experience" is neither the extra-textual experience of a subject placed at the origin of writing nor the experience of a written object conceived as the product of the work of such a subject. Blanchot's "experience"—*the experience of Blanchot*—is the experience of writing understood, itself, as experience. Consequently, Blanchot's reflections on the "experiences of" other writers entangle themselves thoroughly in the reflexive webbing of *the experience of the experience of writing.*[2]

This entanglement begins in the impossibility of determining a subject when it comes to the experience of writing. "To write" says Blanchot, "is to pass from *Je* to *Il,* such that what happens to me happens to no one."[3] This *Il* is not an identifiable third person to whom any writing that happens may be referred. Rather, it remains "uncharacterizable":

> If . . . to write is to pass from *je* to *il, il,* when substituted for *je,* does not simply designate another me any more than it would designate aesthetic

> disinterestedness . . . what remains to be discovered is what is at stake when writing responds to the demands of this uncharacterizable *il*.[4]

Blanchot's *il* is a "third person that is neither a third person, nor the simple cloak of impersonality."[5] Nor does this *neither . . . nor* construction that structures all of Blanchot's propositions concerning the *il* of writing map out any *via negativa* to the positing of a subject. Rather, it obeys the strange logic of "the neutral," the term by which Blanchot names the impossibility of determining the *il* of writing as any subject, whether individual or collective:[6]

> The narrative *il* . . . thus marks the intrusion of the other—understood as neutral—in its irreducible strangeness . . . The other speaks. But when the other is speaking, no one speaks because the other, which we must refrain from honoring with a capital letter that would determine it by way of a majestic substantive, as though it had some substantial or even unique presence, is precisely never simply the other. The other is neither the one nor the other, and the neutral that indicates it withdraws it from both, as it does from unity, always establishing itself outside the term, the act, or the subject through which it claims to offer itself. The narrative voice . . . derives from this its aphony. It is a voice that has no place in the work, but neither does it hang over it; far from falling out of some sky under the guarantee of a superior Transcendence, the *il* is . . . rather a kind of void in the work.[7]

"Neutral" rather than negative, the impossibility of determining the *il* as a subject indicates, for Blanchot, an experience that cannot be understood in terms of the traditional (Aristotelian) logic of possibility:

> But must we not also say: impossibility, neither negation nor affirmation, indicates what in being has always already *preceded* being and yields to no ontology? Certainly, we must! Which amounts to the presentiment that it is again being that awaits in possibility, and that if it negates itself in possibility, it is in order better to preserve itself from this *other* experience that always precedes it and is always more initial than the affirmation that names being. This would be the experience that . . . we are seeking to name . . . in speaking of the *neutral*.[8]

And this "other experience" is the experience of the other, on which, according to Blanchot, *all* experience depends:

> Impossibility is nothing other than the mark of what we so readily call experience, for there is experience in the strict sense only where something radically *other* is in play.[9]

The strict sense of "experience" marked, throughout Blanchot's writings, by "impossibility" departs from the familiar sense in which a subject, as subject, does its dance with an object or with its own subjectivity. Rather, experience of the other as other—"experience" in Blanchot's strict sense—is marked, fundamentally, by the impossibility of saying whether that genitive construction ("experience of the other") is to be read as subjective or objective. And this grammatical ambiguity is inescapable in Blanchot's writing because writing, for Blanchot, is experience, in the strict sense of experience, before it is anything else. Writing is not, first and foremost, the particular sort of work that can be done and does in fact get done by writers. Rather, the first mark of writing, in Blanchot's description of writing, is the "impossibility" that marks experience as experience.[10]

Whenever Blanchot discusses dreaming—and dreaming, along with the night, is an important and recurrent concern in his work—he discusses it in terms of the experience of writing. Just as the *il* of writing cannot, in its otherness, be given the form of a subject, the dreamer of the dream cannot be identified with the conveniently collected figure of the sleeper. In a meditation on Michel Leiris called "Dreaming, Writing," Blanchot thinks this likeness through:

> Who is the "I" of the dream? Who is the person to whom one attributes this "I," admitting that there is one? Between the one who sleeps and the one who is the subject of the dream's plot, there is a fissure, the hint of an interval and a difference of structure; of course it is not truly another, another person, but what is it? And if, upon awakening, we hastily and greedily take possession of the night's adventures, as if they belonged to us, is it not with a certain feeling of usurpation (of gratitude as well)? Do we not preserve the memory of an irreducible distance . . . An intrigue and questioning that refer us to an experience often described of late: the experience of the writer when, in a narrative, poetic, or dramatic work, he writes "I," not knowing who says it or what relation he maintains with himself.
>
> In this sense, the dream is perhaps close to literature.[11]

"To write is to pass from *Je* to *Il*," and dreaming involves the same sort of passage:

> In the depths of the dream—admitting that it has a depth, a depth that is all surface—is an allusion to a possibility of being that is anonymous, such that to dream would be to accept this invitation to exist almost anonymously, outside of oneself . . . a self without self, incapable of recognizing itself as such because it cannot be the subject of itself. Who would dare transfer to the dreamer—be it at the invitation of the evil genius—the privilege of the *Cogito* and allow him to utter with full confidence: "I dream therefore I am"? At most one might propose for him to say, "Where I dream, there it is awake" [*La où je rêve, cela veille*], a vigilance that is the surprise of the dream and where there lies awake in effect, in a present without duration, a presence without person, the non-presence in which no being ever arises and whose grammatical formula would be the *Il* that designates neither this one nor that one. (146/169)[12]

The neutral *Il* wakes in the dream while the subject sleeps. The dream operates according to the same "grammatical formula" as writing. This may explain why the dream so often seems to call for writing:

> The dream is a temptation for writing perhaps because writing also has to do with this neutral vigilance that the night of sleep tries to extinguish, but that the night of the dream awakens and ceaselessly maintains. (147/169)

The dream and writing "have to do" with the same neutral vigilance that continues, in sleep, where the subject leaves off. "Poetry lives on perpetual insomnia," says René Char in Blanchot's approving quotation (147/170). The dream, for Blanchot, is the pure perpetuation of insomnia—"the impossibility of sleeping" (147/170) that we encounter in the very heart of sleep.[13]

This insomniac vigilance is Blanchot's central concern from at least *The Space of Literature* to the last of his writings. By 1968, the concern was widely shared. Utterly restless vigilance (as opposed to the repose of knowledge sought in "totalizing" systematic thinking) became the only acceptable ethical position for the generation of Derrida, Deleuze, and Foucault in its struggle to wake from a thousand metaphysical slumbers. Such an unrestful position can look worn out where it's still held in the present day. Talk of this "vigilance" can seem merely theoretical, especially where it has acquired blackguard habits. But a further look at what the imperative meant for Blanchot may make the matter more naked. For Blanchot, who explores it single-mindedly, "vigilance" is not a grand theoretical attitude but an imperative that we know from the most ordinary experience—the *specific nocturnal experience* of not being able to fully sleep, even in the depths of sleep.

Though Blanchot's exploration of this experience takes many paths, all of these paths return him, in the end, to the myth of Orpheus, which tells, in his reading of it, the first story of the night. The sleeplessness involved in the dream is, as Blanchot tells the story, a requirement of the changed night that Orpheus enters when he turns to see Eurydice.

The Night of Writing

At the center of *The Space of Literature* there is a chapter called "Inspiration." In a note at the beginning of the book, Blanchot directs the reader to the central section of this chapter:

> A book, even a fragmentary one, has a center that attracts it. This center is not fixed, but is displaced by the pressure of the book . . . He who writes the book writes it out of desire for this center and out of ignorance. The feeling of having touched it can very well be only the illusion of having reached it. When the book in question is one whose purpose is to elucidate, there is a kind of methodological good faith in stating toward what point it seems to be directed: here, toward the pages entitled "Orpheus's Gaze" ["*Le Regard d'Orphée*"].[14]

"Writing," says Blanchot at the end of this section, "begins with Orpheus's gaze" (176/232). The object of this gaze is the "essence of the night":

> When Orpheus descends toward Eurydice, art is the power by which night opens. Because of art's strength, night welcomes him; it becomes welcoming intimacy, the harmony and accord of the first night. But it is toward Eurydice that Orpheus has descended. For him, Eurydice is the furthest that art can reach. Under a name that hides her and a veil that covers her, she is the profoundly obscure point toward which art and desire, death and night, seem to tend. She is the instant when the essence of the night approaches as the *other* night. (171/225)

This distinction between the "first night" (or what he elsewhere calls the "night of sleep")[15] and the "other night" models a logic that Blanchot follows in many of his key distinctions (for example, his distinctions between the possible death to the world and the impossible "other" death and between the image as ideal placeholder of an absent object and the image as the visibility not of an absent object but of absence itself).[16] As we saw in the introduction to this book, Blanchot does not oppose the "first night" to the "other night" as contraries, but uncovers the latter "in the heart" of the former in the same way that he finds the "ruin" or the "impossibility" or the "désoeuvrement" of the true work of art to be the central experience and the basis of that work:

> The work [*oeuvre*] of Orpheus does not consist in securing the approach of this point by descending into the depths. His *work* is to bring it back into the light of day. Orpheus is capable of everything, except he can't look at this "point" head on, can't look at the center of the night in the night. He can descend toward it. He can—a power yet stronger—draw it to him and draw it with him upward, but only by turning away from it. This turn away [*ce detour*] is the only way to approach it: such is the meaning of the dissimulation that reveals itself in the night. But Orpheus, in the movement of his migration, forgets the work that he has to accomplish, and he forgets it necessarily, for the ultimate exigency of his movement is not that there be a work but that someone hold himself before this "point," seize its essence there where this essence appears, where it is essential and essentially appearance: in the heart of the night. (171/225–26, translation modified)

In "the heart of the night" is the "other night," and in the heart of the work is the forgetting or loss of the work, of the project of the work, and of its possibility. The "other night" is not the negation of the "first night," and the *desoeuvrement* or impossibility of the work of art is not the negation of the work of art. The otherness of the other in the "other night" and the "impossibility" of the work are to be thought of positively, "in the heart" of the night and of the work. The relation between these terms is therefore not dialectical. The relation is rather one of "duplicité"—an irreducible doubleness that implies, endlessly, deception.[17] Blanchot thus speaks of "the trap of the other night" (168/220, translation modified).[18] It's in the "first night" that we are caught by the "other night." There are no brave literary adventurers in Blanchot setting out in the heroic effort to penetrate to the "heart of the night." Rather, Blanchot's favorite literary figures are led there, not having chosen one way or the other, by the "first night." There's no power and glory to be found in the "heart of the night," only the experience of the impossibility of the work that one has been trying to do, the pursuit of which has brought the writer to this inglorious point:[19]

> The work draws whomever devotes himself to it toward the point where it undergoes impossibility. An experience that is properly nocturnal, that is the very experience of the night. (163/213, translation modified)

This does not mean, however, that the writer in pursuit of his or her work is an innocent and unknowing victim of this entrapment in the nocturnal experience of its impossibility. Blanchot sees, in the literature of his times, an irreversible and potentially paralyzing awareness of this formerly more thoroughly dissimulated essential experience:

> The essential thing to be said about this experience is perhaps as follows: for a long time works went through it, but unknowingly. Or they gave it a name that hid it. That was when art wanted to make the gods present or to represent men. Today it is different. The work is no longer innocent; it knows whence it comes . . . This experience has become so grave that the artist . . . seeks to express it directly or, in other words, *to make of the work a road toward inspiration*—that which protects and preserves the purity of inspiration—*and not of inspiration a road toward the work.* (186/245–46)

The modern work depends, as much as the ancient work, upon inspiration, but upon an inspiration now seen to depend, in its turn, upon the work. This circle of dependence is, as far as logic is concerned, vicious, despite the fact that its ends can never be properly joined. The work can never fully be left (it can't reach or come to coincide with the inspiration it posits as its beginning and seeks as its end), nor can it properly be begun in an inspiration imagined to precede it. "Only the moment of the experience counts" (187/247), but the exact moment of the experience can never rightly be pinpointed as present:

> There is no exact moment at which one would pass from night to the *other* night, no limit at which to stop and come back in the other direction. Midnight never falls at midnight. Midnight falls when the dice are cast, but they cannot be cast till midnight. (169/222)[20]

Thus, though Blanchot can say that "writing begins with Orpheus's gaze"—the turning away from the possibility of the work, in which turning the night discloses "the *other* night"—he can't say when that beginning takes place. There is no identifiable instant when that which precedes writing stops and writing begins, as the experience from which writing springs is already an experience of writing:

> One writes only if one reaches that instant which nevertheless one can only approach in the space opened by the movement of writing. To write, one has to write already. In this contradiction are situated the essence of writing, the difficulty of the experience, and the leap of inspiration. (176/232, translation modified).

The "Movement" in the "Movement of Writing"

"The movement of writing" in the quotation above names the broad and most basic experience of writing, which cannot be reduced to the technical matter of putting pen to paper—to the doing of the work—and which thus cannot, with certainty, be limited to a particular time and place. (One never knows when the midnight of the experience of writing falls, as that midnight must always: (1) have fallen already for writing to begin; and (2) not have fallen yet.) Throughout "Orpheus's Gaze," Blanchot speaks of Orpheus's turn toward Eurydice as his "movement."[21]

In *The Infinite Conversation,* Blanchot dwells on the question of this movement, calling it "the most profound question":

> Language lends itself to the movement of stealing and turning way—it watches over it [*veille sur lui*] . . . Can we at least delimit the experience of this *neutral turn* that is at work in turning away? One of the characteristic traits of this experience is that it cannot be assumed by the one to whom it happens, by a subject in the first person; it only realizes itself by introducing into the field of its realization the *impossibility* of its accomplishment . . . The most profound question is this experience of turning away. (23–24/31–32, translation modified)

This movement in which "writing begins" is the "*uninterrupted* movement of writing" (xxi/xxii) because it cannot itself be assigned a clear end or beginning and thus can indicate no definite end or beginning to the experience of writing. It is "the pure movement of writing" (329/482) because it is defined not privatively, in opposition to rest, but on its own terms, as entirely irreducible to any concept of rest. As pure restlessness—movement irreducible to rest—the movement of writing is the source, for Blanchot's speakers in *The Infinite Conversation,* of a truly endless fatigue. *The Infinite Conversation* begins in this fatigue and takes it as its first theme—the subject of the entire opening dialogue is the fatigue of the two speakers, which makes the conversation *impossible*—but, as one of the speakers duly notes in the course of the impossible conversation, "when he speaks of fatigue, it is difficult to know what he is speaking of" (xx/xxi, translation modified).

Fatigue is an impossible theme—the first sign of the experience marked by "impossibility"—and is thus difficult to explicate. Likewise, the utterly restless movement of which fatigue is the unavoidable companion is difficult to explicate. Indeed, in the existentialist climate in which Blanchot's thinking develops, "movement" is a common name for what most deeply resists systematic, scientific explication. For a central figure and influential teacher like Jean Wahl, existence, in its essential undefinability, *is* movement:

> We have already seen that existence doesn't allow itself to be defined, but we can legitimately characterize it if we say that existence is movement, for we thus define it by something that itself is not defined—movement doesn't allow itself to be defined any more than existence does.[22]

Wahl takes his cue here from Kierkegaard: "For me, all is movement" says Kierkegaard, by way of an exposition of the vanity of systematic knowlege, in which everything might find its final explanation.[23] Kierkegaard's struggle to articulate, against Hegelian conceptualism, the ultimately unconceptualizable movement of existence is rejoined in French philosophy's postwar encounter with Hegel, where it mixes with an old motif in French thinking. "The world," says Montaigne, "is but a perennial see-saw":

> All things in it are in constant motion—the earth, the rocks of the Caucasus, the pyramids of Egypt—both with the common motion and with their own. Stability itself is nothing but a more languid movement back and forth. I cannot keep my subject still. It goes befuddled and staggering, with a natural drunkenness. I take it in this condition, just as it is at the moment I give my attention to it. I do not portray being: I portray passing [*le passage*].[24]

"*Le passage,*" or what thinkers like Jean Wahl will call, following Kierkegaard, "existence."

By the generation of Deleuze, Foucault, and Derrida, Kierkegaard and "existence" are no longer the latest arms in the French struggle with and through Hegelian conceptualism. However, "movement" remains the key bone of contention. Deleuze, for example, in his attempt to conceive difference and repetition in themselves (and not negatively with respect to sameness and the original), constantly opposes "real movement" to "abstract" Hegelian "movement" of the concept. In whatever topic he may be examining at any given moment in *Difference and Repetition,* Deleuze is always searching it for "real movement." For example, discussing Nietzsche and "true theater" Deleuze opposes "repetition as real movement . . . to representation which is a false movement of the abstract."[25] "Theater is real movement."[26] In Derrida's more reserved discourse, what Deleuze thinks of openly as "real movement" is sought in slighter alterations, like that in which an "a" for an "e" makes "différance" in order to name not a concept but a prior *movement* undermining, constantly, the establishment of concepts.

So "movement" or metonymies of "movement" have—from existentialism, to Blanchot, to Deleuze and Derrida—named (or named the trace of, or have given the trace of a name to) the positivity of what can't be explicated conceptually. This "movement" is fatiguing. As Blanchot describes it, the experience of the restless "movement of writing" is an experience of the deepest fatigue. Talk of it—"theory"—becomes too tiring for words if the dream, to which it refers, is entirely forgotten.

The Dream as Movement and Mise en abîme

Already in Aristotle, for whom all movement can be referred either to a violent displacement of something from its natural place or to the natural tendency of things toward restful position in their natural places, the dream is understood as a kind of movement that sleep cannot still. For Aristotle, the dream represents the continuation of the movements of sense impressions received in waking. He compares these movements to those of projectiles in space, "for in the case of these the movement continues even when that which set up the movement is no longer in contact."[27] Though these movements of the dream cannot be brought to rest in sleep, they can, for Aristotle, be safely assigned a clear beginning in the sense experience of daytime, which, in turn, can be understood in terms of his physics, in which all motions begin and end in rest. For Blanchot, who writes in a post-Copernican universe in which "natural place" no longer has any meaning and in which the fundamental Aristotelian concept of rest has long since been replaced by that of *inertial movement,* the old thought that the dream is a kind of movement becomes unsettling because the movement that the dream represents can no longer be said to begin and end in rest. The dream comes to represent the very endlessness of inertial movement and the impossibility of resting, even in sleep.

In Aristotle's distinction between the dream and sleep, the dream represents the continuation of the movements of the day, whereas sleep is essentially a nocturnal matter. In Blanchot's post-Copernican following through of the same basic distinction, the situation is inverted: sleep is now essentially an extension of daytime concerns, whereas the restless movement of the dream is essentially nocturnal:

> What happens at night? Generally we sleep. By means of sleep, day uses night to blot out the night. Sleep belongs to the world; it is a task. We sleep in acccord with the general law that makes our daytime activity depend on our nightly repose. We call upon sleep and it comes . . . Sleeping is the clear action that promises us to the day . . . Only deep sleep lets us escape what there is in the deep of sleep. Where is the night? There is no longer any night . . . You must sleep: this is the watch-word that consciousness assigns itself, and this commandment to renounce the day is one of day's first rules.
>
> Sleep transforms night into possibility.[28]

The essence of the night—the "other night" in the heart of the night—is "impossibility." Possibility is a matter of the light of day. Sleep, as a recharging of one's powers for the purposes of day, turns the night to the purposes of day. We remain tightly "attached," in sleep, to the day:

> It is an attachment, in the affective sense of this term: I attach myself, not like Ulysses to the mast with bonds from which later I would like to free myself, but through an agreement expressed by the sensual accord of my head with the pillow, of my body with the peace and happiness of the bed. I retire from the world's immensity and its disquietude, but in order to give myself to the world, which is maintained, thanks to my "attachment," in the sure truth of a limited and firmly circumscribed place. Sleep is my absolute interest in assuring myself of the world. From this limit which sleep provides, I take hold of the world by its finite side; I grasp it firmly enough so that it stays, puts me in place, puts me to rest. To sleep badly is precisely to be unable to find one's position. The bad sleeper tosses and turns in search of that genuine place . . . The sleepwalker is suspect, for he is the man who

> does not find repose in sleep. Asleep, he is nevertheless without a place and, it may be said, without faith. He lacks fundamental sincerity, or, more precisely, his sincerity lacks foundation. It lacks that position he seeks, which is also repose.[29]

Sleep, in the sincerity of its attachments, resists the "duplicity" of the neutral "speech of writing," whose speaker cannot be reduced to any locatable "I" or grouping of "I's":

> I sleep. The sovereignty of the "I" dominates this absence that it grants itself and that is its doing [*son oeuvre*]. I sleep: it is I who sleep and none other.[30]

In sleep, the sleeper collects him or herself, for the sake of the enterprises of the day, into a single position, a resting place in which he or she is a grounded and grounding subject, at home in the world.

In Blanchot's conception of sleep and dreaming, the night (every night) frustrates, in the form of the dream, this project of restful grounding:

> Night, the essence of the night, does not let us sleep . . . In the night one cannot sleep.
>
> One does not proceed from day to night. Whoever follows this route finds only sleep—sleep that ends the day but in order to make the next day possible . . . In this sense the dream is closer than sleep to the nocturnal region. If day survives itself in the night, if it exceeds its term, if it becomes that which cannot be interrupted, then already it is no longer day. It is the uninterrupted and the incessant . . .
>
> The dream is the awakening of the interminable.[31]

"The interminable," "the uninterrupted," "the incessant": there's more than a little theatricality involved in these Blanchotian substantivizations of adjectives, and the "Voilà!" tacit in these gestures obscures as much as it puts in view. What is "the interminable," after all? What is "the incessant" in itself, beyond this or that failure to stop? "Real movement" or "pure movement beyond rest," strange names themselves, do at least clearly designate what can't be substantively defined. But awkward adjectival appelations come with the nocturnal territory in which Blanchot is operating. All of these weak half-namings are a function of Blanchot's strong claim that what dreams the dream is not recognizable, and therefore namable, as a subject:

> He who dreams sleeps, but already he who dreams is he who sleeps no longer. He is not another, some other person, but the premonition of the other, of that which cannot say "I" any more, which recognizes itself neither in itself nor in others.[32]

Who or what dreams cannot be dragged into the light of day and stopped for identification. What dreams the dream is the incessance of the movement of the dream. The dream is, as it was for Aristotle, movement. However, the dreamer is not the subject of this movement—who or what moves or is moved—but its essential quality, "incessance." The dreamer, "he who dreams," is a feature of the dream.

Thus Blanchot's dreamer cannot be said to exist outside the dream. This account of the dream would tally with traditional skeptical accounts if it did not rigorously distinguish the dreamer from the sleeper. Though the dreamer cannot be said to exist outside the dream in Blanchot's account, neither can the dream be located inside the mind of any sleeper. The space of the dream is that of "the outside," which Blanchot points to as the central "space of literature" throughout his writings (the central chapter of *The Space of Literature*—"Inspiration"—begins with a section called "The Outside, The Night"). In this respect, Blanchot is closer to the Homeric, mythological tradition than he is to Aristotle's psychologism. Though in Blanchot the dream can no longer be said to come through the gates of horn, from the gods, from demons, or from the dead, and though it can no longer be said to appear at the foot of the sleeper's bed—in the literal outside space of the bedroom—its space remains outside and not inside the mind of the sleeper. The endless *mise en abîme* structure of the dream without subject does not lock the dreamer in, cutting the dreamer off from contact with the outside.[33] On the contrary, in Blanchot's account of the dream, the dreamer is locked out and therefore radically exposed to "the outside which has no location and affords no rest."[34] This "outside" to which the *mise en abîme* structure exposes us is, says Blanchot, "the region where pure resemblance reigns":[35]

> Everything there is similar; each figure is another one, is similar to another and to yet another, and this last to still another. One seeks the original model, wanting to be referred to a point of departure, an initial revelation, but there is none. The dream is the likeness that refers eternally to likeness.[36]

In Blanchot, this region without resting place or point of departure is the region of the image.[37]

Dream, Writing, and the Image

In *The Space of Literature*, Blanchot tries to develop a concept of the image founded upon "pure resemblance"—"a resemblance which has nothing to resemble" (260/350). Blanchot's model for the image no longer subordinated to a model that precedes it is the corpse. In the corpse, Blanchot observes, "the mourned deceased begins to *resemble himself*" (257/346). This resemblance of the deceased to himself is not, principally, a resemblance of the deceased to himself in life, but rather to himself as deceased:

> Himself: is this not an ill-chosen expression? Shouldn't we say: the deceased resembles the person he was when he was alive? "Resembles himself" is, however, correct. "Himself" designates the impersonal being, distant and inaccessible . . . Yes, it is he, the dear living person, but all the same it is more than he . . . so absolutely himself that it is as if he were *doubled* by himself. (257–58/346)

This doubling adds something—"all the same it is more than he"—that can't be reduced, in any way, to the object doubled. What is added, in the case of the corpse-image, is the positive absence of "the dear living person":

> The image can certainly help us to grasp the thing ideally—it is the life-giving negation of the thing—but at the level to which the weight that is proper to it pulls us, it also threatens constantly to carry us back not to the absent thing but to absence as presence, to the neutral double of the object. (262/353, translation modified)

The corpse is not only an image of an absent object ("the dear living person") but also an image of the absence of the object. This latter version of the image (the latter of what Blanchot calls "the two versions of the imaginary") is not subordinated to the former.[38] On the contrary, for Blanchot the image as image is first and foremost the image of image—the image as presentation of absence itself, which, in itself, is image. First and foremost, "the corpse is its own image" (258/347, translation modified). In this more radical of the "two versions of the imaginary," the corpse is, in itself, the image of a corpse, which is to say the image of an image of an image ad infinitum. This endless, groundless structure is, for Blanchot, that of resemblance itself, defined on its own terms and not according to those of the logic of the representation of objects:

> And if the corpse bears such a resemblance [*est si ressemblant*], it is because it is, at a certain moment, resemblance itself, entirely resemblance, and nothing more. (258/347, translation modified)

For Blanchot, this pure resemblance (resemblance without object) is pure movement (movement without rest). "Subjects" and "objects" take up positions in the world—they are posed and therefore capable of repose. In the more radical of Blanchot's "two versions of the imaginary," the corpse, as pure resemblance, is *not an object* and cannot be said to be at rest:

> We dress the corpse, and we bring it as close as possible to a normal appearance by effacing the hurtful marks of sickness, but we know that in its ever so peaceful and secure immobility it does not rest. The place that it occupies is drawn down by it, sinks with it, and in this dissolution attacks the possibility of a *dwelling place* even for us who remain . . . The belief that at a certain moment the deceased begins to wander [*errer*] . . . must be understood as stemming from the premonition of the *error* that now he represents. (259/348–49)

In the very extremity of the immobility of the corpse understood as an object, the corpse appears as the objectless image of itself and thus as errant movement—the very image of the "suspension of the relation with place" that is death:

> Death suspends the relation to place, even though the deceased rests heavily in his spot as if upon the only basis that is left him. To be precise, this basis lacks, the place is missing, the corpse is not in its place. Where is it? It is not here, and yet it is not anywhere else. Nowhere? But then nowhere is here. (256/344)

The restless "movement of writing" is a function of this same suspension. The "movement of writing" is not the movement from place to place of any object but rather the movement of an image as image. In a long footnote to the first section of *The Space of Literature,* Blanchot defines literature as the image of language:

> In literature, doesn't language itself become altogether image? We do not mean a language containing images or one that casts reality in figures, but one that is its own image, an image of language (and not a figurative language), or yet again, an imaginary language, one that no one speaks; a language, that is, which issues from its own absence, the way the image emerges upon the absence of the thing; a language addressing itself to the shadow of events as well, not to their reality, and this because of the fact that the words that express them are not signs but images, images of words, and words where things turn into images. (34/31–32)

He then worries that this definition of literature as image might seem to imply that writing is secondary to the speech it represents:

> What are we seeking to represent by saying this? Are we not on a path leading back to suppositions happily abandoned, analogous to the one that used to define art as imitation, a copy of the real? If, in the poem, language becomes its own image, doesn't this mean that poetic language is always second, secondary? According to the common analysis, the image comes after the object. It is the object's continuation. We see, then we imagine. After the object comes the image. "After" seems to indicate subordination. We really speak, then we speak in our imagination, or we imagine ourselves speaking. Wouldn't poetic language be the copy, the dim shadow, the transposition—in a space where the requirements of effectiveness are attenuated—of the sole speaking language? But perhaps the common analysis is mistaken? Perhaps, before going further, one ought to ask: but what is the image? (34/32)

By the end of *The Space of Literature,* Blanchot will have answered that the image is essentially pure, objectless resemblance. This answer makes it possible to define writing as the image of language without falling into the subordination of writing to speech that that definition of writing traditionally entails. Writing—"the poem"—is an image of language in the same way that the corpse is the image of itself. "The poem" doesn't represent language from the outside, as a prior object. Rather, language is given in it, not as an object to be represented, but as "its own image," the image of the objectless image that it is. Writing, the image of language, is, in this analysis, involved inseparably in language from the beginning because, in the beginning, language is image and not object.

"Literature . . . language that no one speaks" cannot be neatly cordoned off from spoken language. "Literature," through its relation to the image, comes to name a silent dimension of language in general. The intellectual problem that this "literature" presents is not limitable to a particular field of knowledge, defined in terms of its object. As Blanchot defines it, the problem of literature is the broader and more general problem of the restlessness of the corpse—the restlessness of the image as image even, and especially, in the very image of final rest.

For Blanchot, dreams—the images that are somehow ours in sleep—involve all of us, nightly, in just this restlessness. And in Blanchot's image of this generally shared restlessness, the common analogy, as old as mortality itself, between the sleeping body and the corpse is reconfigured. Traditionally both are figures of rest—the one provisional and the other final (unless one believes in resurrection, in which case the difference between death and sleep is largely elided). This remains the case in Blanchot. However, Blanchot reads these exemplary figures of rest *ironically*—as extreme indications of the ultimate impossibility of rest. We have seen that Blanchot conceives of the dream as restlessness in the heart of sleep—the impossibility of fully sleeping that presents itself in sleep. Full sleep, sleep without images (without dreams), would be death, which, though *like* sleep in the analogy, is not sleep. The possibility of sleep is thus the impossibility of full sleep, or death, in sleep. The corpse, as image of itself, is, in Blanchot's analysis, itself restless, despite the extreme rest that it represents in the world of objects. Though death is not sleep in Blanchot, the impossibility of rest is the same in sleep and in death: the restlessness, in sleep, of the dream and, in death, of the corpse is a result of the same "impossibility of death."

Just as there are "two versions of the imaginary" in Blanchot, there are two versions of death.[39] The first is death to the world—the *vale* that one has in one's power and that one can accomplish in suicide. The second is the impossible death—the death that one does not have in one's power as a subject to accomplish. This death, though it indubitably happens (the impossible does, without fail, happen in Blanchot), does not happen to "us" or to "me" or to "you" or to any other possible subject of the happening, as it is the very absencing of the subject of its happening. No one can, as subject, be said to be present and "there" for his or her own death, in this sense of "death." "What happens to me" when death, in this sense, happens "happens to no one."[40] Dreams, the images that happen in sleep, can be said to happen "to the sleeper" in only the same limited sense in which death can be said to happen "to the body." The death that happens "to the body," which, unlike the subject, is *there* in death, is not the impossible death for which the subject cannot be present. In its restlessness, the dead body—the corpse-image—is, in Blanchot's analysis, the image of the absence of the subject of that death and not, in any way, an image of the subject of the experience of death. Likewise dreams, in Blanchot's account, are images of the absence of the subject of the experience of dreaming. Though, upon the return to life signalled by waking up, the likeness of the latter absence to the former might seem to be undone, the cognate absence of the subject in writing—in the general, limitless, and therefore inescapable experience of writing that Blanchot explores—carries the restlessness of the dream, in the form of the image of absence, past the return to life, through the day, and back into the night, the center of which—the source of all restlessness—is, as we have seen, the "impossibility" that marks experience as experience in Blanchot's account. "Awak'd you not in this sore agony?" asks the Keeper of the Tower in Shakespeare's *Richard III*, interrupting Clarence's account of his dream of death. "No, no," Clarence replies, "My dream was lengthened after life."[41]

Dream, Writing, and Disaster: Veiller

"I call disaster," says Blanchot, "that for which the ultimate is not a limit."[42] In *The Writing of the Disaster*, Blanchot names the impossibility of resting in sleep, and even in death, "disaster." In the dream, as in death, "the subject becomes absence" (51). What speaks in this absence—what, in *The Infinite Conversation*, Blanchot calls "the speech of writing"—is now named "disaster." Instructing himself in the writing of this "subjectivity without subject" (124), Blanchot tells himself, toward the beginning of *The Writing of the Disaster*, "It's not you who will speak; allow the disaster to speak in you" (12). Though such speech may be "allowed" or accepted to a greater or lesser degree, it is not in one's power in such a way that it can be willed or even wanted: "To want to write, what an absurdity:

writing is the downfall of the will, just as it is the loss of power, the fall of the cadence, the disaster again" (24). The writing of the disaster is thus not writing that one desires and does as a project in the world, and, therefore, it is possible that it may never, in fact, get done: "When to write or not to write is without importance, then writing changes—whether it happens or not, it is the writing of the disaster" (25). But whether or not any writing actually gets done, the writing of the disaster goes inescapably on: "Not to write—an effect of writing" (23). The verb that Blanchot everywhere employs to name this restless going-on without beginning or end is "veiller"—to wake, stay up, keep watch, stand vigil:

> The watch [*la veille*] has neither beginning nor end. "Veiller" is neutral. "I" don't wake [*"Je" ne veille pas*] . . . It wakes [*Cela veille*] . . . The disaster wakes. (82)

"If I say: the disaster wakes, it is not in order to give *la veille* a subject" (85)—Blanchot issues such cautions at every turn of *The Writing of the Disaster.* The genitive construction of "the writing of the disaster"—the writing of this *veille*—thus cannot be determined as indicating either an objective or a subjective sense. The disaster, *la veille,* is not a subject of writing, nor is it an object to be written "about" by any subject. It names what we've seen Blanchot call, in earlier writings, "the movement" of writing itself. Though this movement goes on beyond the willing and doing of any subjects, it remains, somehow, a responsibility: "However, it's necessary to keep watch over [*veiller sur*] the measureless absence, watch without cease" (134). Though one does not "do" this writing—though one cannot, as subject, wake or be vigilant in this necessary way—this writing, this waking, is nonetheless our responsibility. Everyone is implicated in this writing/waking precisely because it is not the doing of this or that particular subject. In this generally shared implication, Blanchot sees "the exigency [*exigence*] of a thinking that surrenders to the multiple and seeks to escape the inflation of the One" (196). This exigency does not determine a responsibility *for any subject* and thus cannot be understood in juridical terms. It is rather "the lawless exigency [*exigence sans droit*] of the other" (198). The surrender of thought to the multiple does not occur in the light of any right or any law. Rather, it is a surrender to the lawless night. For Blanchot, the starry night represents the universe—a unity—with its laws and its order. The disaster, "night free of stars," is a "multiple night" (13).

"*White night, night without sleep—such is the disaster*" (8). The disaster, night without stars, is a night without sleep—the night not of sleep but of the dream, which, as we've seen, Blanchot defines as the impossibility of sleep. The writing of the disaster is the writing of the dream, and, in the irreducible ambiguity of that genitive ("writing of the dream"), the dream may be thought of as a kind of writing in which everyone (everyone dreams) is involved every night. Blanchot's definition of writing as objectless image in *The Space of Literature* opens the way for this line of thinking, as dreams are likewise images that can't be subordinated to objects. But the way in which we are responsible for this kind of writing (for our dreams) remains largely unexplored—just as largely unexplored as the ways, beyond the juridical, in which we are responsible for all of the disasters of our times, the ceaseless images of which are generally either mistaken for objects or decried, by those who claim to know, as the making imaginary of "real" objects of knowledge. In this general subordination of the image to the object, the tendency when it comes to literature is to look at writing in only its objective senses, quietly slipping Blanchot's dreamier sense of writing into the long sleep of intellectual history.

But sleep is not death, though it may look like it, and the irreducible difference between the two is the dream. This difference is the easiest thing in the world to forget, as the experience of every morning shows. Remembering it calls for a vigilance beyond the familiar kind that begins its watch only upon waking and ends it at the moment of falling asleep. Though nothing in Blanchot's obsessive pursuit of it makes a "vigilance" that crosses the frontier of sleep feel familiar, and though it retains an oxymoronic ring in his discourse, nothing in Blanchot removes it from the ordinary either. At the end of the day, Blanchot may or may not succeed in remembering the dream, but either way, by locating the vigilance needed in order to remember the dream in the very heart of the dream—by defining the dream *as* nocturnal vigilance—Blanchot insists that remembering the dream is remembering, among other things, that there is no special distinction in being vigilant. Everyone dreams, and Blanchot's strange talk of nocturnal vigilance brings us back, in the end, to that. The verb in the final complete sentence of *The Writing of the Disaster* is "share"—"let us share [*partageons*]" (220). This imperative comes not from the deathly heights of the tower of the law, where Shakespeare's Clarence sleeps, but from the common depths of our nightly experience of the impossibility of fully resting, from the bottom of the sea of Clarence's dream.

THREE

Beckett's Restlessness

Going On Without Rest and the Problem of the Time of Writing

Writing is the center of the action in Beckett's trilogy (*Molloy; Malone Dies;* and *The Unnamable*). The comic energy of Molloy's account of his journey to see his mother is derived not from the slow unfolding and ultimate dissipation of the action of that journey in space but from the fits and starts of the unfolding of his writing in a strange present in which the journey is both over and not over. From his mother's room he writes: "But now I do not wander any more, anywhere any more, and indeed I scarcely stir at all, and yet nothing is changed."[1] In Part II of *Molloy,* what Moran says in the past tense of his search for Molloy holds as well for the present in which he writes out his report:

> What I assert, deny, question, in the present, I still can. But mostly I shall use the various tenses of the past. For mostly I do not know. (105/143)

> For in describing this day I am once more he who suffered it . . . And as then my thoughts would have none of Molloy, so tonight my pen. (122/165)

> I am far more he who finds than he who tells what he has found, now as then. (133/181)

Malone, for his part, writes—in his notebook, on his putative deathbed, with his pencil—inventories and fables of his life in an attempt to be done with it. Any stories from the past and other inventions that may appear are convoked to this central scene. And the unnamable narrator of the last book of the trilogy, hearing only the flimsiest rumors of a foregoing life "in the light," narrates instead the action of his own speaking, which, though it no longer clearly involves implements, is still somehow writing:

> How, in such conditions, can I write, to consider only the manual aspect of that bitter folly? I don't know. I could know. But I shall not know. Not this time. It is I who write, who cannot raise my hand from my knee. It is I who think, just enough to write, whose head is far. I am Matthew and I am the angel, I who came before the cross, before the sinning, came into the world, came here.[2]

Each of Beckett's speakers in these works wants to be finished with this writing with which they all are tasked, whether or not they ever "raise their hands from their knees" to write (in the sense of the "manual aspect" of the verb "to write"): "that's what counts, to be done, to have done."[3] But finishing is impossible, as "the search for the means to put an end to things, an end to speech, is what enables the discourse to continue."[4] Going on means stopping ("it was the only way to progress, to stop," says Molloy of his strange movements on his endless journey home, which are and aren't the movements of the unfolding of his writing in his mother's room, where he both is and isn't), and stopping means going on.[5] Writing must go on in order to finish and finish in order to go on. Thus, even in the impossible silence astonishingly allowed for in the last words of *The Unnamable,* there is no end to writing but the equally impossible continuation of it:

> You must say words, as long as there are any, until they find me, until they say me, strange pain, strange sin, you must go on, perhaps it's done already, perhaps they have said me already, perhaps they have carried me to the threshold of my story, before the door that opens on my story, that would surprise me, if it opens, it will be I, it will be the silence, where I am, I don't know, I'll never know, in the silence you don't know, you must go on, I can't go on, I'll go on.[6]

Taken out of context, these famous last words of *The Unnamable* can be taken to express a brave decision to persevere against all odds and in the face of despair. Much of Beckett's celebrity is owed to this sort of mistake, by which Beckett, cast in the role of hero of the human spirit, is made to bravely show us what it might mean to carry on in spite of the inhumanity of it all. But Beckett is scrupulous in avoiding all flattery of the human being and hard on humanist critics of art: "With 'It's not human,' everything's said. To the garbage. Tomorrow it will be demanded of sausages that they be human."[7]

In his critical writings on art, Beckett makes plain his frustrations with the persistence of the idea that art is supposed to "express" what is human—especially human powers and possibilities. Against an art of exploits in the domain of the humanly possible, Beckett dreams "of an art turning from it in disgust, weary of puny exploits, weary of pretending to be able, of being able, or doing a little better the same old thing, of going a little further along a dreary road."[8] In his critical "dream of an art unresentful of its insuperable indigence," Beckett celebrates his friend Bram van Velde for his "fidelity" in painting to "the failure" of painting.[9] Though painting may discover a thousand new objects to paint and a thousand new ways to paint them, at bottom "there is nothing to paint and nothing to paint with," though the painter remains, nonetheless, "obliged to paint."[10] So the strange responsibility of painting cannot be described in terms of "the old subject-object relation," in which painting is conceived as representing objects that precede it or as expressing subjectivities that underlie it.[11] The persistent, inscrutable obligation to paint can be answered only by carrying out "the mourning of the object [*le deuil de l'objet*]" and not by recourse to any subjects or objects "to be painted."[12]

As it is for painting, so it is for writing in Beckett. The unnamable last speaker in Beckett's trilogy is, like the painter of Beckett's "dream of an art unresentful of its insuperable indigence," obscurely obligated to go on speaking, which is, "in such conditions," to go on writing, though he doesn't have anything to say or write, or anything to speak or write with.[13] In the embraced indigence in which this writing goes obligatorily on, the absence of any preexisting condition to be represented or expressed is so thorough that even death can't be thought of as implying a preliminary life:

> However this may be, and without dwelling further on these macabre details, it is certain I was grievously mistaken in supposing that death in itself could be regarded as evidence, or even a strong presumption, in support of a preliminary life.[14]

Speaking with admiration of the painting of Geer van Velde (Bram's brother), Beckett makes clear his sense, as a writer, of a shared situation with the painters van Velde:

> Here everything moves, swims, flees, returns, undoes itself, remakes itself. Everything ceases, without cease.
>
> That's what literature is.[15]

In the absence of outside fueling (subjects to express or objects to represent), the cessation that naturally results when fuel runs dry turns, in the first paradox of Beckettian art, to fuel for further fuelless going on.

Beckett gives us no encouragement to think of the speaker's faring forward at the end of *The Unnamable* ("I can't go on, I'll go on") as the brave exploit of a human subject exercising his free and sovereign will in a freely made decision to persevere, the limitations be damned. Were such a thought to occur to the unnamable speaker himself (it doesn't), it's impossible to imagine that he wouldn't nip it in the bud: "Decide?" he would ask, "but *with what*?"[16] There's a kind of heroism in his immunity to any impulse to glamorize his predicament, but it's certainly not the decisive kind. The unnamable speaker goes on speaking at the end of *The Unnamable*—goes on writing, though he knows not how—simply because stopping is as impossible as going on in a situation where "everything ceases, without cease." If decision in the matter were in any way in his power, he would certainly have stopped from the start. Going on is an unavoidable imperative, as unavoidable as the imperative of stopping, and there can be no particular distinction in obeying because there is never any question of there being even the slightest choice in the matter.

In its maddening impossibility, the situation of a speaker confronted with these contradictory imperatives may seem far out of the ordinary—it might seem like the special predicament of the madman or of the great writer. But the situation of Beckett's strange speakers is as strangely ordinary as it is impossible. Though Beckett's speakers might roll in the mud like St. Francis, and though, in their poverty and thoroughgoing literal-mindedness, their comedy borrows heavily from that of the saints, they never float, fly, or transcend in any of the ways that saints might.[17] Nor do they plummet to sublime depths, though the indefinite spaces that Beckett opens have often been glamorized as "hells" of one kind or another. Neither saved nor damned, Beckett's speakers in the trilogy occupy something like the purgatorial position of the first of Beckett's characters, Belacqua of *Dream of Fair to Middling Women* (a novel of 1932, unpublished in Beckett's lifetime) and *More Pricks than Kicks* (a collection, published in 1934, of stories mostly culled from the novel).

Dante's Belacqua is a comical and unexceptional figure, neither here nor there. Though he has done nothing but rest, he is too exhausted to climb the mountain of purgatory and remains, head between his knees, in the shade of a boulder at the foot of the mountain.[18] In turning to him in *Dream*, Beckett turns to a comic image of the paradoxical restlessness that Freud and Blanchot study in their explorations of dream-life—restlessness in the very depths of rest. This is not the unmitigated unrest of hell, but it's not paradise either. Belacqua's hardly laborious but nonetheless restless search for rest unfolds in a neither here nor there that doubles the here and now (he has to remain in purgatory for exactly the length of his lifetime).[19]

For Beckett's restless idlers, to rest—paradise—would be to find the origin of their discourse. In the trilogy, Beckett's speakers relentlessly press permutations of one question: "Who, in the final instance, is speaking here?" No response ever sticks. One theory always leads to another, right down the line to *The Unnamable,* which names not the end of the line but its endlessness. In the absence of a figure at its end, this line cuts across the border between the world of Beckett's characters and the world in which the reader holds *The Unnamable* in his or her hands. Their restlessness reveals itself as ours, a general concern.

Resisting this generalization of a particular textual condition, the reader might seek rest where Beckett's characters can't, outside the fiction, in the solid knowledge that a real person named Samuel Beckett is really at the bottom of all of this talk of restlessness—its ultimate and exemplary sufferer. Because Beckett's self-reflexive fictions present this restlessness as a writing problem, we might imagine that the problem belongs only to the writer and not to the reader—that the writer wrestles heroically with a special restlessness from which the reader may remain free. But not writing or not having written doesn't free the reader from the writing problem Beckett presents any more than the unnamable speaker of *The Unnamable* is freed from writing by having nothing to write with in the way of paper or an implement or even a hand.

The writing problem with which Beckett confronts us is not a technical problem, not a difficulty or occupational hazard of the craft pursued by writers (a small elite), who try, with ink and paper, to produce writings. Nor is it an allegorical *mise en scène* of a putatively extra-literary problem like the absurdity of existence.[20] Beckett's characters who write, without quite knowing how, are ironic figures for the author—the writer, in the technical sense, of the work. There would be no irony in these figures if the technical distinction of the author completely disappeared in the drawing of them, but the figures would not be as articulate as they are if they didn't speak for the author in writing without any of the usual marks of this distinction. Shadowing closely the creatures of his writing as they move from link to link in a chain of speakers that can't end at the end of the story that posits it, Beckett follows the steps of a strange logic by which everyone is implicated in writing (not only those who write, in the technical sense of the verb). According to this logic, general unrest has a literary form.

As a technical question, the writing of the trilogy can be circumscribed in time and space. We know that Beckett wrote it and we know the approximate time and place. But the strange present of the unfolding of the writing in the trilogy cannot be circumscribed in this way. Beckett's writings, the main action of which is writing itself, brandish the difference between the temporality of writing and (1) the temporality of performance (say, singing at a certain hour at a certain place *Nacht und Träume* by Schubert, a song after which Beckett named one of his television pieces)[21] and (2) the temporality of production (say, cobbling a shoe).

In the case of the performance, the singing of the song happens at a determinate place and time. If the singer stops singing in the middle of the song, that constitutes a problematic interruption in the performance of the song. Even in the technical sense of committing ink to paper, the writing of a work is not like this sort of performance, as it happens in fits and starts, and usually at many different times and in different places. And in the essential and more than technical sense of "writing," there is no way of saying, with any exactitude, when writing begins and when it ends. Wallace Stevens is said to have composed poems, doubtless after long gestation, "in his mind," dictating them to his secretary upon arrival at work. Proust leaves us no way whatsoever of positively saying where the *recherche* for the work ends and the writing of *La Recherche* begins, as *La Recherche* was in *la recherche* from the start and vice versa. Coleridge claims to have received *Kubla Khan* in a dream. And then there's the extreme and therefore paradigmatic case of Homer. In all cases, one cannot say exactly when the writing happened. And in the case of Homer, it never happened, in the technical sense of committing marks to a writing surface. Homer didn't write his works, in the technical sense of the verb, but he can still be counted as a writer. When *The Odyssey* becomes, through transcription, a work of writing in the technical sense of the word, it makes sense to say that Homer wrote it, while it doesn't make sense to say that the technicians who transcribed it "wrote" it.

As for production, in the example of cobbling a shoe, cutting the leather into pieces of the proper size and shape, and stitching those pieces together *is* the making of the shoe, and one can measure precisely the time spent in these activities (the temporality of the designing of a shoe would be a more complicated matter). Analogies between writing and productive activities like cobbling are common currency in the rhetoric of literature and of literary criticism, but there is a limit to how close these analogies can be. The joining of letters together into words and phrases cannot be said to happen "in ink, on the page" in the same way that the joining together of pieces of leather into a shoe is the coming into being of the shoe. Literary joining can be done "in one's head" or in one's soul in a way that the joining of a shoe cannot because the basic stuff of language is not like leather. This difference in materiality makes traditional metaphors of the psyche as a writing surface both resonant and aberrant; writing does happen in the soul in a way that cobbling doesn't, but the analogy between soul and paper is meaningful only because of the deep, material difference it both elides and implies. The production of a mark on the page (or in the sand, or on the screen) can be timed. But, as anyone who has ever sat in front of a blank page knows, writing resists commitment to the page as much as it demands it. The actual time of the commitment of the mark to the page can be measured, at least in theory, but the resistance essential to it makes the time of the real labor much more strange—a long night of the soul, whatever the actual hour of the spilling of the ink.

So, though performance and production can be said to happen between the hours of x and y, writing cannot be said to happen in the same way. Throughout *The Unnamable*, the time of writing—the present of the unfolding of the speech of the unnamable speaker who, in speaking, somehow writes without literally writing—is called "this evening." But, because Beckett is writing about the event of writing and not about subjects, objects, or experiences presumed to precede writing, time words like "evening" spread, change, and slip into "dawn" when he writes them:

> In the evening air, it's evening, that's all I know, evening, shadows, somewhere, anywhere, on the earth. Go mad, yes, but there it is, what would I go mad with, and evening isn't sure either, it needn't be evening, dawn too bestows long shadows, on all that is still standing, that's all that matters, only the shadows matter, with no life of their own, no shape and no respite, perhaps it's dawn, evening of night, it doesn't matter.[22]

Such a mutable evening of writing can stretch on indefinitely. But the center point over which it stretches remains fixed. Between the ordinary evening of day and the "evening of night" lies midnight, the time without present set for writing *qua* writing by Mallarmé, whose settings have pretty much held for all subsequent self-reflexive literature.[23] Moran famously begins his account—Part II of *Molloy*—at this temporal turning point: "It is midnight. The rain is beating on the windows."[24]

In Part I of *Molloy*, Molloy, like the unnamable speaker of *The Unnamable*, has been busy mixing up day and evening. Like his descendant or ancestor in *The Unnamable* (the logic of the succession of Beckett's characters is no more clear than that of his times of day), Molloy writes in a time he calls "this evening":

> Lousse was a woman of extraordinary flatness, physically speaking of course, to such a point that I am still wondering this evening, in the comparative silence of my last abode, if she was not a man rather. (56/74–75)

Ordinary distinctions between times like "this evening" and times like "days" have little hold in Molloy's telling of the time:

> And I am quite willing to go on thinking of her as an old woman, widowed and withered, and of Ruth as another, for she too used to speak of her defunct husband and of his inability to satisfy her legitimate cravings. And there are days, like this evening, when my memory confuses them and I am tempted to think of them as one and the same old hag. (59/78)

This happy confusion of "day" and "evening" transmutes to high anxiety and, ironically, to high style in the indeterminacy of the time of writing in Moran's account, which extends the "evening" of Molloy's writing into a "morning": "But this evening, this morning, I have drunk a little more than usual" (132/180). The midnight at which Moran begins his account splits what's left of the difference between these times.

Moran's son sleeps soundly at this hour, but Moran can't, and writing is, it seems, the unavoidable concomitant of his inability to sleep: "My son is sleeping. Let him sleep. The night will come when he too, unable to sleep, will get up and go to his desk. I shall be forgotten" (92/125). Moran says he's calm ("I am calm. All is sleeping."), but this is clearly not the case. The order from above (from Youdi via Gaber) to go out in search of Molloy has interrupted his "day of rest" (92/125). He describes his last minutes before receiving his orders to pursue Molloy as his "last moments of peace and happiness" (93/126), and he writes his report under the terrible pressure of those orders.[25] Under this pressure, he will have need of morphine, to which, what's more, he seems to have had habitual recourse before receiving his pressing orders concerning Molloy.[26] "Quiet Moran, Quiet. No emotion please [*Allez, Moran, du calme. Pas d'émotion, de grâce*]" (132/180), he interjects to himself as goes.[27] Finally, he openly confesses, in a despairing exclamation, the anxiety that dogs the present of his writing: "Oh the stories I could tell you if I were easy [*si j'étais tranquille*]" (137/187). But this outburst brings him more distress than relief. Only one page later, he tries to contain it by projecting his anxiety onto the reader, whom he tells to be tranquil, even though it is not at all clear what reason the reader would have not to be:

> And we would have peaceably pursued our way on foot, but for the following incident.
>
> One night, having finally succeeded in falling asleep beside my son as usual, I woke with a start, feeling as if I had just been dealt a violent blow. It's all right [*Soyez tranquille*], I'm not going to tell you a dream properly so called. (138/188)

Why on earth should the reader fear the recounting of a dream? And why on earth would the reader even anticipate the recounting of a dream here, where the occurrence of a bona fide violent event is, in view of the build-up preparing us for a "following incident," entirely to be expected, especially in light of the entirely matter of fact murderousness encountered in the wilderness of Part I?[28] Of course, what follows is the recounting neither of an event nor of a dream, "properly so called." Moran wakes up in debilitating pain on account of his knee, though he finds it to be neither red nor swollen. His son is fast asleep, and there's no sign whatsoever that any violent event has occurred outside the world of his dreams. There's some possibility that the pain isn't entirely new, but Moran can't remember; he remembers that one of his knees hurt on the day of his departure, but he can't remember which one. In any case, even if the pain isn't new, there's no explanation for its debilitating intensity, which will require that Moran send his son, once he wakes up, to the town of Hole to buy the Mollovian bicycle that is his destined post-ambulatory means of going on.

There is no good scientific explanation for Moran's pain, yet it should have subsided upon waking had the blow that caused it been received in a dream. We wouldn't have feared a story of blows received in a dream "properly so called," but Moran's narrative of this strange, nocturnal "incident" is another story. And in telling us not to fear what we wouldn't have known to fear had he not mentioned it, Moran makes us look to the dream for the source of his pain. His insistence that we "be tranquil" communicates the deep unrest that only a dreamless sleep—a sleep closed to the blows of experience—could interrupt. Whether directed to his readers or to himself, Moran's frequent calls for calm are entirely anxious—spurring more of the unrest by which they're spurred—and hilarious. Laughter is the closest one will come to rest in Beckett's fiction, which tells few dreams but registers the kind of blow that a dream can bring.

Moran's calls for calm mark a rhythm without rests in the strange time of writing in which dawn and evening cannot be distinguished. In this time, it cannot be true to say "it is x or y o'clock"; unlike the time of performance or of production, the time of writing is, as we've seen, not measurable in this way. And yet such things continue to be said in Beckett's writing in the spirit of pure and necessary fiction ("when you have nothing left to say you talk of time, seconds of time")[29]—not the sort of fiction in which one is supposed to "believe" for a time, as in an alternate reality, but a fiction beyond belief, which cannot be safely returned, like a flight of fancy, to some point in reality (in "real" historical time, for example) from which it can be said with confidence to originate. Such fiction cannot be undermined, as undermining it only uncovers more of it. Thus, at the end of Moran's report, when the "It is midnight" of the beginning of the report is revealed, along with the driving rain, to be just a matter of writing—pure fiction—it is not to point to a truer or more accurate account of the writing situation underneath the "lie" of "midnight" and of the rain:

> I have spoken of a voice telling me things . . . It told me to write the report. Does this mean I am freer now than I was? I do not know. I shall learn. Then I went back into the house and wrote, It is midnight. The rain is beating on the windows. It was not midnight. It was not raining. (175–76/238–39)

"It is noon. Sunlight is streaming into the room" would have been equally false. Any precise time and any precise description of the weather at the beginning would have been equally false because the time of the end is not strictly separable from the time of the beginning,[30] and we, like Moran, can't know in the end if Moran is any freer than he was in the beginning from the tyranny of the voice that mandated the "false" beginning. (We "shall learn" in the subsequent books of the trilogy that, in fact, he isn't.) The interlacing of the beginning and the end makes for a complex and layered time in which it can never be any one hour and in which the weather can never be any one way. In the end, the opening description of the time of the writing of the report is incorporated, through citation, into the past of the narrative ("and [I] wrote, It is midnight"). But this gesture, by which the circle of the story is closed, does not end the story in such a way as to free—for a more accurate and truthful description—the present of the time of writing from the fictional chains of the past of the narrative.

The time and weather noted in the final sentences of *Molloy* are the same both in the fictional situation, in which a figure named Moran exposes the fictions in which his writing was begun, and in the "real" situation, in which Beckett is exposing the fictions (like that of a report-writer named Moran) in which his writing was begun. In neither was it midnight and in neither was it raining. And from the point of view of neither do these final sentences, though grammatically negative, negate or pull the rug out from under the first sentences of Moran's report.

In writing, Beckett and Moran share a general situation in which fictional lives and times (like Moran's "midnight") cannot be returned to any real lives and times (like Beckett's days and nights of 1947) any more than the latter can depart or escape into the former. It wasn't midnight, and it wasn't raining, not because it was some other time and the weather was different, but because writing necessarily puts forth pure fictions.

Writing as Quotation Without End ("I say it as I hear it")

The entire length of Moran's report—Part II of *Molloy*—separates the claim that "it is midnight" from the retraction of that claim. In *The Unnamable*—the final book of the trilogy—the space between affirmation and denial narrows, as the discourse there proceeds according to an accelerated and ever-accelerating rhythm of x, not x, y, not y. This speed of the alternation in the discourse, which has increased in inverse proportion to that of the physical movements of the speakers—who, never highly mobile, are now to be found in nearly complete paralysis—expresses a crisis of conviction that comes with the territory of pure fiction. In *The Unnamable*, which represents the farthest reaches of this territory, fictional first-person speaker and author collapse, not the one into the other, but both into an unnamable figure that is neither one nor the other, nor, for that matter, another *one* of any kind. Though this unnamable figure says "I" in the way that any namable speaker might, he can't believe what he says. So, from the very beginning of the book, saying "I" is followed immediately by a retraction:

> Where now? Who now? When now? Unquestioning. I, say I. Unbelieving [*sans le penser*] . . . I seem to speak, it is not I, about me, it is not about me.[31]

Mirroring the recursive structure of Moran's report, the speaking of these words at the beginning of *The Unnamable*—"say I. Unbelieving"—is *mise en abîme* at its end: "In the end it comes to that . . . the words come back, someone says I, unbelieving" (402/192–93). In this return of the words of the beginning of the book, the "I" said or implied in every sentence of *The Unnamable* turns out to be like Moran's "midnight" and "rain"—pure fiction, beyond belief. That is, to disbelieve this fiction is not to find it false vis à vis something truer. The speaker does not disbelieve with a truer "I" than the "I" in which he disbelieves. Though resolute in its negativity—vigilant in immediately denying its every "I"—this way of expressing disbelief is not a viable *via negativa* to a hidden "I" to whom the assertion of disbelief might be safely attributed. The "I" of *The Unnamable* is thus an "I" that cannot know its way, though it knows it's been this way before:

> What am I to do, what shall I do, what should I do, in my situation, how proceed? By aporia pure and simple? Or by affirmations and negations invalidated as uttered, or sooner or later . . . the yesses and noes . . . they will come back to me as I go along and how, like a bird, to shit on them all without exception. (291/7–8)

From beginning to end, *The Unnamable* pursues the most meticulous account of this "situation" in which "I" can be said only in disbelief. The unnamable speaker is relentless in his investigation of conditions that, calling for investigation, call upon him to continue speaking—conditions that cannot, he discovers again and again, be considered conditions of possibility. A sense of unquestionable obligation drives this self-reflexive discourse: "Having nothing to say, no words but the words of others, I have to speak" (314/46). The strange implication is that he would not be obligated to speak in the same pressing way if he had something to say in his own words. He is obligated to speak as a subject—to say "I"—but he is subject to this obligation precisely because "I" isn't he (turning the question around, the speaker often wonders whether he shouldn't therefore say "he" instead of "I"). The unnamable speaker is obligated to speak not despite his alienation from his own words but because of it—

because the words that he speaks, starting with the first-person singular pronoun, cannot be his.

In the past, the speaker has experienced this obligation as the dictation of a domineering, singular other named Mahood (né Basil):

> I'll call him Mahood . . . It was he told me stories about me, lived in my stead, issued forth from me, came back to me, entered back into me, heaped stories on my head. I don't know how it was done. I always liked not knowing, but Mahood said it wasn't right . . . And still today, as he would say, though he plagues me no more his voice is there, in mine, but less, less. And being no longer renewed it will disappear one day, I hope, from mine, completely. But in order for that to happen I must speak, speak. (309/37–38)

As this speech unfolds, as the tale is told, Mahood fades, and we hear more from and about a less determinate "they":

> What I speak of, what I speak with, all comes from them . . . To testify to them, until I die, as if there was any dying with that tomfoolery, that's what they've sworn they'll bring me to. (324/62–63)

The names the speaker has taken in the past are theirs. He disowns these names. But the disowning of them is also theirs:

> I am neither, I needn't say, Murphy, nor Watt, nor Mercier, nor—no, I can't even bring myself to name them, nor any of the others whose very names I forget, who told me I was they, who I must have tried to be, under duress . . . I never desired, never sought, never suffered, never partook in any of that, never knew what it was to have, things, adversaries, mind, senses. But enough of this. There is no use denying, no use harping on the same old thing I know so well, and so easy to say, and which simply amounts in the end to speaking yet again in the way they intend me to speak, that is to say about them, even with execration and disbelief. (326/65)

"Do they believe I believe it is I who am speaking? That's theirs too" (345/98). Any expression the unnamable speaker might produce under these circumstances can belong only to "them." There is some possibility, however, that some non-expressive features of the speaker's discourse may belong to him—for example, the poor quality of his quotation. Though he can speak only by quotation, he doesn't necessarily quote *well* what's dictated to him to say: "I say what I am told to say . . . The trouble is I say it wrong [*Seulement je le dis mal*], having no ear, no head, no memory" (345/98). And then there's the crucial matter of the slight delay between what he hears and what he says:

> I shall transmit the words as received, by the ear, or roared through a trumpet into the arsehole, in all their purity, and in the same order, as far as possible. This infinitesimal lag, between arrival and departure, this trifling delay in evacuation, is all I have to worry about [*j'en fais mon affaire*]. (349/104)

Surprisingly, in something like the way he finds himself "in the silence" in the last lines of the book, the unnamable speaker sometimes finds himself directed toward something like himself in the "infinitesimal" space between the heard and the said:

> Between them would be the place to be, where you suffer, rejoice, at being bereft of speech, bereft of thought, and feel nothing, that would be a blessed place to be, where you are. (374/145–46)

> They'll have said who I am, and I'll have heard, without an ear I'll have heard, and I'll have said it, without a mouth I'll have said it, I'll have said it inside me, then in the same breath outside me, perhaps that's what I feel, an outside and an inside and me in the middle, perhaps that's what I am, the thing that divides the world in two, on the one side the outside, on the other the inside, that can be as thin as foil, I'm neither one side nor the other, I'm in the middle, I'm the partition . . . I'm the tympanum. (383/160)

But then there come, in equal measure, reminders that even this silence in-between is given by "them" as pauses in "their" discourse:

> The dirty pack of fake maniacs, they know I don't know, they know I forget all they say as fast as they say it. These little pauses are a poor trick too. When they go silent, so do I. A second later, I'm a second behind them, I remember a second, for the space of a second, that is to say long enough to blurt it out, as received, while receiving the next, which is none of my business either. Not an instant I can call my own. (368/136)

These reminders that he has next to no sovereignty do not, however, strengthen the speaker's sense of the sovereignty of the dictating "they." On the contrary, the more the difference between the heard and the said is narrowed, the closer to "them" the speaker feels himself to be. In this proximity, the paranoid hypothesis of a dictating "they" loses its hold on the rhetorical situation. Toward the end of the book, the unnamable speaker advances a bold new hypothesis:

> Assume notably henceforward that the thing said and the thing heard have a common source, resisting for this purpose the temptation to call in question the possibility of assuming anything whatever. (390/172)

This shift in the speaker's assumptions begins in the thought that "they" do not speak any more freely than he does. Like him, "they" labor under the interdiction of any rest in speaking: "But they are compelled to speak, it is forbidden them to stop" (371–72/141). And because they can't stop, it is impossible to say where "they" stop and "I" begins:

> I hear everything, every word they say, it's the only sound, as if I were speaking, to myself, out loud, in the end you don't know any more, a voice that never stops, where it's coming from. (369/137)

Unable to pause for thought, "they" can no more stand behind the thoughts that the unnamable speaker expresses than he can: "they make me say, If only this, if only that, but the idea is theirs, no, the idea is not theirs either" (376/148).

We might take this leveling of the hierarchical distinction between "they" and "I" as evidence that the real subject of the voice of *The Unnamable* is a grand collective: "we." But the unnamable speaker has considered this theory and sees no more sense in it than he sees in any of the others: "Who, we? Don't all speak at once, there's no sense in that either" (360/123). In this situation of pure quotation—of speech unattributable to any subject, first-person or third, singular or plural—hearing and speaking cease to be functions determined by the positions of this or that subject but become dual functions of a voice without subject: "the voice listens" (408/203). From within the nonetheless unavoidable pronominal "bickering" over the distribution of subject positions, the joining of these functions can only be imagined as taboo—as a masturbation scene in which subject and object are problematically "confused":

> In the meantime no sense in bickering about pronouns and other parts of blather. The subject doesn't matter, there is none. Worm being in the singular, as it turned out, they are in the plural, to avoid confusion, confusion is better avoided, pending the great confounding. Perhaps there is only one of them, one would do the trick just as well, but he might get mixed up with his victim, that would be abominable, downright masturbation. (360/123)[32]

From the perspective of the habitual logic of subject–object relations, "masturbation" is a confusion always to be put off, left for the future, "pending the great confounding." But *in flagrante delicto*—in the delight of the self-reflexivity or auto-eroticism of a voice without subject—the great confounding cannot be considered a future event. "Death," says Wittgenstein, "is not an event of life."[33] The subject cannot be present for it. Confounding the ordinary temporal order of speaking and listening, the "voice that listens" confounds as well the ordinary temporal order of life and death: it speaks already from the experience of death in speaking in the absence of any subject. If the voice didn't come, in this sense, from the future (not from a future present but from a pure future in the present), the otherwise unbelieving speaker of *The Unnamable* would not for a moment be able to believe in his death. And, though his belief is never firm, at moments he can in fact lightly affirm it. He cannot for a second affirm any belief in the "I," which must absent itself at the moment of death, but he can say that he "believes" in the silence of death, despite having no feeling whatsoever for death as fatality—as a necessity inscribed in the natural order of things:

> I'll drown for good, then the silence, I believe it this evening, still this evening, how it drags on, I've no objection, perhaps it's springtime, violets, no, that's autumn, there's a time for everything, for the things that pass, the things that end, they could never get me to understand that, the things that stir, depart, return, a light changing, they could never get me to see that, and death into the bargain, a voice dying . . . on we go (409/203–4)

This lightly held belief in his future silence is a further expression of his disbelief in the "I" said or implied in his every sentence. It's in this very silence that the "I" rings hollow. Where the subject is absent, the silence of the end is already there. It's there in his absence at the origin of the words he says. The unnamable speaker must go on speaking even though he can't go on because the silence he seeks is not external to speech. If it were, both speaking and ceasing to speak would be entirely possible for him. Speaking is impossible for him precisely because it goes on "in the silence"—because the silence he seeks, the absolute end of speech, is immanent to it.[34] The speech presented in *The Unnamable* is not endlessly restless because it knows no stopping but rather because stopping is part of it, a manner of speaking: "never easy [*jamais tranquille*], always stopping" (318/53). "The comma will come" (409/203), quotes the unnamable speaker. Not a full stop.

But must we share the unnamable speaker's disbelief in any "I" that might pass his lips? Is the end of which he speaks in his endless quotation the one that attends us all? Don't we see what the unnamable speaker cannot, namely that Samuel Beckett is the ultimate source of all of this speech?

Certainly, the state of affairs described by the unnamable speaker is a fiction posited within the fiction writing of Samuel Beckett, and our knowing this leads to many dramatic ironies. However, "Samuel Beckett" cannot, by virtue of the undeniable fact of his authorship of his fiction, be cited as the ultimate source of all of the quotation in *The Unnamable,* its true and nonfictional alpha and omega. Indeed, it is precisely because Samuel Beckett is the subject in question throughout all of *The Unnamable*'s questing after a subject—because no other subject of the discourse can be named—that "Samuel Beckett" cannot be cited in this way. Samuel Beckett is the question, not the answer.[35]

In seeking beyond ready answers for the source of all the speech it quotes, *The Unnamable* plumbs the depths of the second-handedness of language. "High" modernist citational style had already specialized in this sort of plumbing, but not without aggrandizing the plumber in the process. Beckett studiously avoids this kind of self-aggrandizement. His ever-deepening sense of the fundamental and not in any way secondary second-handedness of language—a traditional word for which would be "tradition"—calls for no "individual talent" charged, by this heightened sense, with exceptionally "great difficulties and responsibilities."[36] For a "high" modernist like T. S. Eliot, quotation and allusion convoke literary tradition to a strange present in which "past" writing is changed by "present" writing just as much as the latter is influenced by the former.[37] In this bargain, which Hugh Kenner, following Wyndham Lewis, thinks of as an exchange of time for space—a matter of what Kenner calls "spacecraft"— modern poets join ancient poets in the glorious contemporaneousness of a cliquish renaissance:

> Literary history as the Romantics apprehended it, today's poems near, yesterday's far, the year before yesteryear's yet farther, Greek things exceedingly remote: this romance of temporal distance is simply absent. As in *The Lives of the Poets* all poets are contemporaneous, though not merely the poets a

common idiom unites: the poets, of whatever date or language, whose clean perception sets realities before the mind.[38]

Though all speech under the conditions presented in *The Unnamable* proceeds by quotation and therefore unfolds in the strangely limitless present ("this evening" that is not an evening) of the time of writing, no pantheon-like space of living monuments is thereby erected, into which Beckett might enter, quoting. Though the time of writing exposed in Beckett cannot be assimilated into the normal morning, evening, or night time of the world, that stubborn difference cannot be made to serve as a basis for any literary elitism of writer-figures who, especially aware of "great difficulties and responsibilities" bestride, obliged by *noblesse,* the whole infinitely suffering world in writing. On the contrary, in Beckett's extension of the principle of modernist citational style to every dusty corner of his speech, the difference between the time of writing and the normal time of the world is the "difficulty and responsibility" of everyone. If Molloy, Moran, Malone, and the unnamable speaker share it, then who doesn't share it? These motley writer figures who share with Beckett the "I" said without belief are clearly not to be numbered among the poetic elect, and Beckett, by virtue of the "I" that he shares with them, shares in their lowliness, which cannot in any way be glamorized (neither as sanctity nor as damnation nor as madness).

Though the lowly come forward and past and future are confused in Beckett's endlessly unfolding quotation, Beckett does not thereby present us with an apocalyptic time in which the last are first. The low are not raised by his sharing of their fate any more than he descends to join them. Neither alpha nor omega, he starts and ends where his lowly writer-figures start and end—not in the originality of any logos capable of ever being or ever having been fleshed out but in an endlessly secondary and endlessly shared voice. In *How It Is*—his first extended work of fiction after *The Unnamable,* produced after nearly a decade of hard delay—this voice is heard in the mud. Face down in the mud, the speaker hears what is now called the "quaqua on all sides" in "bits and scraps" and repeats back to the mud ("I quote," he says, quoting, at every turn) what he hears in it.[39] Returning after nearly a decade to the impossible dictates of the irreducibly plural voice that last dictated the wild promise to go on at the end of *The Unnamable,* Beckett returns us to the mud of the common ground that his fiction discovers and rediscovers—mud that is primal precisely because language awaits us and outlasts us in it. Face down in it, language comes to us.

The speaker in *How It Is* doesn't know how it is that he knows how to speak the words he hears in the mud, but one explanation he hears and repeats is that he has learned them from the writing, carved with a fingernail on his body, of a companion, whose role the speaker will assume, in his turn, in the second part of his "journey." According to the basic fiction heard and spoken (and, in the process, endlessly permutated, complicated, and contradicted) in the mud of *How It Is,* the speaker's journey comprises four parts: (1) the journey to Pim, his companion–victim; (2) time with Pim, on whose body he, as Pim's "tormentor," carves his name and other imposed locutions, which, a victim once himself, the speaker has learned likewise on his body; (3) time after Pim, in which, abandoned by Pim, he awaits the arrival of his own "tormentor"; and (4) time of victimage at the hands of Bom (according to one rumor in the mud), who will again teach him to hear and speak by writing, with his nails, on his body.[40] "Sam" is certainly not excluded from this succession of characters bearing one-syllable names ending in "m": "Bom Bem one syllable m at the end all that matters."[41]

Without pen and paper and without any good account of how this speaking that is happening is also the writing that the reader is reading (though less than coherent rumors of a pair named "Krim and Kram," witness and scribe, are heard from time to time in the mud), the speaker in *How It Is* is left to hear and speak of writing as a general clawing that everyone does and has done to them in the mud—the most basic and desperate grasping at contact with others. Clawing and clawed, Beckett asks how it is with himself and how it is with everybody else in the same breath—the same breathless but deep breath in which his speakers ask how it is that what they are saying is writing.

FOUR

Finnegans Wake

An "Ideal Insomnia"

The "quaqua on all sides" that Beckett's speakers distantly hear in the mud and whisper back to the mud in which they hear it echoes a call that *Finnegans Wake* makes to its readers (and to the birds): "Quoiquoiquoiquoiquoiquoiquoiq!"[1]

Joyce's "Quoiquoiquoiq . . ." is the answer of Shem, Sham, Shames (James),[2] a Stephen Dedalus–like figure for the writer in *Finnegans Wake* (seen here in the person of Mercius), to the accusation, thrown at him by his brother Shaun (seen here in the person of Justius),[3] that Shem's pen creates nothing, originates nothing, and does nothing but kill. Concluding his accusation, Shaun/Justius satirically takes the bone of contention (Shem's pen) into his own hands in order to give a demonstration of its infertility: "He points the deathbone and the quick are still" (193). Shem/Mercius responds by returning his brother's gesture with a flourish:

> He lifts the lifewand and the dumb speak.
> —Quoiquoiquoiquoiquoiquoiquoiq!

Though the dumb—in the figure of a seagull or perhaps an ocean duck flying toward the mouth of the Liffey[4]—may indeed be made to speak through Shem's gesture here, that speech is only an echo of the bottom line of his brother's accusation ("What does this mean?" "What have you made?" "What have you done?"—"Quoi, quoi, quoi?"). The echo gives no answer to the question. The only thing the echo adds is a shift in tone, by which the question is turned into an exclamation. Shem/James has no voice of his own, but his echoing of the voices of others introduces ironies into the tones of those voices. Accusation becomes celebration in the "shamebred music" (164) of this ironic echoing, just as questioning becomes exclamation.[5]

Writing, as Socrates complained, cannot respond to questions posed to it.[6] But writing has never thrown questions back at its questioners with as much energy as *Finnegans Wake*. No text has ever produced more bafflement. Hardly indifferent to questioning (despite its inability to respond), the *Wake* sends back the interpreter's questions with a vigor that begs a further question: where is this vigor coming from? That is, who or what, in the end, is speaking here? But no speaking subject can ultimately be made responsible for the text's "Quoiquoiquoiquoiquoiquoiquoiq!" Full of such exclamations and full of historical presents, onomatopoeia, and the most extreme exuberances of free indirect discourse, the text presents us with an uncanny (because subjectless) *enargeia* that, suggesting a living presence, makes us forget, against all evidence, what Socrates knew about writing.

Maintaining all of this *enargeia* takes precisely the kind of energy that Beckett's speakers have been sapped of, though their drive remains stunningly unaffected. There's a manic strain in the tone of Joyce's "quoiquoiquoiq." In Beckett, the "quaqua on all sides" is a depressive murmuring. Quoting it back into the mud that both muffles and transmits it, Beckett's speakers repeat not a grand exclamation but a rhetorical question. Faced with the imperative, face down in the mud, to go on (writing, speaking, thinking), they ask and ask again "avec quoi?"[7] The mania in Joyce's "quoiquoi" was bound to come to this. There's nothing ideal about the situation of Beckett's speakers, but in their inability to find the rest they seek, they embody the real fatigue that the "ideal reader" of *Finnegans Wake* would feel. Giving the *Wake* to readers, Joyce wishes an "ideal insomnia" upon them:

> And look at this prepronominal *funferal*, engraved and retouched and edgewiped and puddenpadded very like a whale's egg farced with pemmican as were it sentenced to be nuzzled over a full trillion times for ever and a night till his noddle sink or swim by that ideal reader suffering from an ideal insomnia.[8]

This "prepronominal *funferal*" is ALP's letter, which stands here for the whole of *Finnegans Wake*, in which speakers can never be firmly identified as "hes," "shes," or "its" with namable antecedents. As a tough egg to crack (the letter is written by an "original hen" [110], sometimes named Biddy Doran) the *Wake* requires that its reader "nuzzle" it not forever and a day but "for ever and a night." The addition of this "night" makes forever look longer than it would look with an added "day" because spending a night at any task—even a task so pleasant as "nuzzling" a text—means losing sleep, in which time flies. But sleep means death when it comes to this "night" beyond forever. Joyce's wish that the reader spend time beyond forever with the *Wake* is not unkind. The insomnia that he wishes upon his reader does not necessarily imply the loss of any actual night's sleep, and it may imply a kind of triumph over death. In that sense it's "ideal." But the unrest it implies is real.[9]

Complaining about the writing of his brother Shem/Mercius (and, with it, the writing of the *Wake* as a whole), Shaun/Justius ridicules the idea of this ideal insomnia: "He points the deathbone and the quick are still. *Insomnia, somnia somniorum. Awmawm*" (193).[10] For Shaun, Shembred "insomnia" is just another name (*in nomine . . .*) for dreams, or worse, for "dreams of dreams" (*somnia somniorum*), for ever and ever (*in secula seculorum*): "Aw Mom [that mixed with a big yawn], tell Shem to stop." And the complaint of Shaun/Justius is, though merciless, just. The experience of waking to which *Finnegans Wake* calls its reader is more like a dream than it is like the real ordeal of the real insomniac, who will in fact catch some sleep here and there. An ordinary night's sleep is a doorway to it.

The Wake *and the Dream: An Approach to Reading*

Faced with a new kind of literary enigma, the first critics of *Finnegans Wake* developed, on the cues of the author himself, the interpretive scheme through which the book is still most often seen. According to this scheme, the elusive subject of the *Wake* is, in one way or another, "a dream." In his influential early review, Edmund Wilson presents the book as "The Dream of H. C. Earwicker."[11] Like Wilson, Harry Levin thinks of the *Wake* as "Earwicker's dream," though he leaves the meaning of this claim a bit more open than does Wilson, who is more concerned with giving a picture of the plot lines of "the dream."[12] Clive Hart agrees that *Finnegans Wake* presents a dream but takes issue with Wilson's "unwarranted assumption" that Earwicker is the dreamer, citing the judgment of Harriet Shaw Weaver, Joyce's patron and literary executrix, that the *Wake* is not "one character's dream" but that the dream in the *Wake* is "a convenient device," giving Joyce "the freest scope" for his writing.[13] Weaver's claim, seconded by Hart, that the *Wake* cannot be thought of as the dream of "one character" coheres with Joyce's famous statement to the journalist Ole Vinding that "there is . . . no connection between the people in *Ulysses* and the people in *Work in Progress* [the working title of *Finnegans Wake* during the 17 years of its composition]":

> There are in a way no characters. It's like a dream. The style is also changing, and unrealistic, like the dream world. If one had to name a character, it would be just an old man. But his own connection with reality is doubtful.[14]

For Hart, "the whole of *Finnegans Wake* is a dream," and any dreaming characters that may appear in it thus dream dreams within a dream.[15] Accordingly, the dreamer of the *Wake* "must always be considered as essentially external to the book, and should be left there":

> Speculation about the "real person" behind the guises of the dream-surrogates or about the function of the dream in relation to unresolved stresses of this hypothetical mind is fruitless.[16]

For Hugh Kenner, "dream" is a way of naming this absence of "reality" behind all of the guises upon guises in the *Wake*. In Kenner's account, "we are not for a moment tempted" in reading the *Wake* "to suppose that we ought to be seeing a subject through a style."[17] The reader's attention is rather directed toward "what is never quite real . . . things that only exist at the suggestion of words."[18] "Joyce's subject: the nullity behind the words, the reality in the words."[19] For Kenner, the *Wake*, in presenting speech behind which no real and original speaking subject can be found, presents a "dream-world":

> In the dream-world of *Finnegans Wake* the mind is detached from responsibility toward things, cut loose in the nowhere—the not quite trackless nowhere in which words remain. It can occupy only the points other minds have occupied before, and can get from one point to another only along the track ripped through space by a quotation, or the fading trail of an *idée reçue*.[20]

In the decades since this first generation of *Wake* criticism, some frustration with the received wisdom that the *Wake* presents us, in one way or another, with "a dream" has emerged. Poststructuralist critics like Derek Attridge, eager to wake from "the dream of meaning" in which criticism imagines that it can decide what, in the final instance, the *Wake* is about, have argued that all the talk about dreams says more about the dreams of anxious critics than it does about the *Wake*.[21] From his position at the helm of the "Joyce industry," Bernard Benstock also calls into question the "easy conclusion that '*Finnegans Wake* is a dream,'" reversing his earlier opinion on the subject.[22] Meanwhile, John Bishop radically revises the classic theory, arguing that, though the *Wake* does represent a particular night's sleep of one gigantic sleeper, dreams only come and go during that sleep. According to Bishop, the *Wake* represents a night much of which is spent in "dream-void sensory paralysis."[23]

Whether expounding new or used versions of the generally accepted dream theory, deconstructing it, flatly contradicting it, or subtly amending it, scholars of Joyce have had to contend with the strong influence of Joyce's own accounts of his book, largely offered in a strategic spirit in response to Harriet Shaw Weaver's polite but thorough skepticism and Ezra Pound's less polite blast of total incomprehension.[24] Joyce's response, in a letter to Miss Weaver, to the first appearance of grave doubts in his old allies has become famous:

> I sent ∧abcd to E.P. at his request and he has written turning it down altogether, can make nothing of it, wading through it for a possible joke etc. . . . yesterday took to the sofa again. Today I restarted. One great part of every human existence is passed in a state which cannot be rendered sensible by the use of wideawake language, cutanddry grammar and goahead plot.[25]

From this moment on, Joyce would "explain" his book, usually in a highly defensive way, by reference to the "world" of night. For example:

> To Ernst Robert Curtius: "The night world can't be represented in the language of day."
>
> To William Bird Joyce: "About my new work . . . I can't understand some of my critics, like Pound and Miss Weaver for instance. They say it's *obscure*. They compare it, of course, with *Ulysses*. But the action of *Ulysses* was chiefly in the daytime, and the action of my new work takes place at night. It's natural things should not be so clear at night, isn't it now?"
>
> To Ole Vinding: "Having written *Ulysses* about the day, I wanted to write this book about the night."[26]

Though such "explanations" are never to be trusted when it comes to literature and ought to be trusted even less coming from such a notoriously tricky horse's mouth, they do, in fact, *work*. If they didn't, they'd pass out of use. Despite his dissent from the prevailing theory that *Finnegans Wake* is a book "about" the night and therefore either "is like," or "is," or is "about" a dream, Derek Attridge underlines the "productivity" of the theory:

> I would prefer to emphasize how productive the idea of the dream has been, in spite of its inadequacies as an interpretive frame, in creating an audience for one of the most complex of all literary texts, and in allowing commentary to flourish in the face of a work that might have been greeted with silence.[27]

The critical talk of dreams by way of "explanation" of the *Wake* illustrates particularly well how the question of what "works" or is "productive" in such explanations is to be separated from the question of whether such explanations truly explain anything, as nothing could offer less stable ground for understanding than the nightworld entered through dreams, about which we still know next to nothing. Had Joyce emphasized instead that the *Wake* is about the vicissitudes of daily life in a bourgeois family (which it is), or had he stuck with his earlier presentations of the work as a "history of the world"[28] (modeled on Vico's *New Science*, as *Ulysses* is modeled on the *Odyssey*, the *Wake* is, in terms of its genre, at least as much a "universal history" as it is a "novel"), or had he offered some version of the often adduced critical truism that the *Wake* is "about language," he would have explained more about his work. The bourgeois family, the history of the world, and language offer, for all of their mysteries, more stable objects of knowledge than the dream. If the *Wake* is the unknown term, any of these terms might function as knowns (or at least more knowns) in terms of which the *Wake* might be at least in part explained.

In his "explanations" of *Finnegans Wake* as an account of the dream-state that holds sway in the nightworld ("One great part of every human existence is passed in a state which cannot be rendered sensible by the use of wideawake language, cutanddry grammar and goahead plot"), Joyce thus offers no more of an answer to the question "what is this about?" than Shem offers with the "Quoiquoiquoiq!" that he gives in response to his brother's complaints about the ultimate insubstantiality of his writing. Joyce, for all of his real eagerness to control the reception of the *Wake,* knew (despite the Parnell fantasies he explores throughout his writing) that he was a writer (and not, for example, a politician or public speaker) as surely as that can be known (how else could he have persisted, for 17 years of modern and not monastic time, in the writing of a wildly unprecedented work for which he received little real encouragement); thus he could not, by way of an explanation, even attempt to answer questions about his writing "better" than his writing can answer questions. And, as Socrates made clear a long time ago, writing is defined by its complete inability to answer questions—to explain itself—in the way that a live speaker can. In pointing, in the guise of an explanation, to the nightworld of dreams—in offering, in the place of an explanation, a term less known than the term it's meant to explain—Joyce is pointing to this basic fact of writing and asking his readers to read.

Any reader of the *Wake* is necessarily involved, at every turn, in "a wake"—a waking of some kind. Among all the uncertainties, *that* is one sure thing. We've seen that talk of dreams offers no sure thing and thus explains little. This does not mean, however, that all the talk of the *Wake* as a dream is false. It only means that the *Wake* will tell its reader more about the dream than any theory of the dream will tell him or her about the *Wake.*

Waking, to the Letter (Thoughtless Speech in the Wake*)*

The word "wake" names many things at once in the title of *Finnegans Wake*: Irish waking of the corpse; staying awake in the night; following in the wake of a fallen giant (and of everything that could ever possibly have been new under the sun); and waking up from sleep. And this use of the word "wake" models the use of all words in the *Wake.* From its title forward, the *Wake* stirs the manyness of meaning, not to dissolve the many into any deeper one, nor to keep the many meanings in suspense in such a way that "the reader is free to choose" the one he or she prefers, but to make the many legible as such:

> (Stoop) if you are abcedminded, to this claybook, what curios of signs (please stoop), in this allaphbed! Can you rede (since We and Thou had it out already) its world? It is the same told of all. Many. Miscegenations on miscegenations. Tieckle. They lived and laughed and loved and left. Forsin.[29]

The writing on the wall (MENE, MENE, TEKEL, and PARSIN from Daniel 5:25) doesn't entirely lose its magic in this parody of it. But where the magic had been that of the oneness of the one God, the parody makes the first magical word "many."

In its systematic punning and mass-production of portmanteaux, the *Wake* celebrates the manyness of its every word, turning on its head the melancholy wisdom that, because human languages are essentially many, they can reflect only fragments of the full richness of thought (a richness of which the dream is often taken to be an emblem). The *Wake* represents a refusal to accept that you can't tell it all—that the better part of a thought must remain latent in anything said in any human tongue—but the "all" it aims to tell in its parody of every single thing anyone might possibly single-mindedly say is not a lost oneness, not an original whole, but the many in all of its manyness. This is parody, after all. Telling it all in this way does not make manifest a fully integrated thinking subject, finally at one with its thoughts. On the contrary, the more the *Wake* succeeds in making thought manifest in all its multiplicity, the more thoughtless its discourse becomes. Chased from its traditional positioning in the secret space behind what is said, a thinking subject comes into the light, but in that light it's a shadow of its former self.

In the thoughtless speech that results from the stunning success of the *Wake*'s attempt to represent thought fully in speech, letters—the senseless elements of literature—come to play (again, the "prepronominal *funferal*") in the vacated place of the thinking subject. Perhaps, as many critics have argued, we are confronted in the *Wake* with the thoughts (in a dream, maybe) of "H.C. Earwicker." But the only steady presence of "H.C. Earwicker, a publican" beneath the multiplicity of his manifestations in the book is "HCE"; each manifestation is an acrostic on these letters. This "publican" has, in the end, no private individual existence:

> It was equally certainly a pleasant turn of the populace which gave him as sense of those normative letters the nickname Here Comes Everybody. An imposing everybody he always indeed looked. (32)

And, without any private individual existence, the "publican" cannot be said to possess any "thoughts of his own." Thoughts given in his name are second-hand thoughts behind which the imposing figure of "Everybody" looms (amidst rumors of a mythic giant named "Finn"-something) in the deserted place of the thinking subject. The thoroughgoing second-handedness of the thoughts of "HCE" is a function of the echoing natural in such a deserted place. "HCE" means "Hush! Caution! Echoland!" (13) just as much as it means "H.C. Earwicker."

In the thoughtlessness of the saying of everything in the *Wake*, letters like "HCE" take precedence over (and do not merely graphically precede) any figures of speech and thought that they might initialize. Thoughts initialized in this literary way can come out quite jumbled, as key distinctions lose their underpinnings. "Tragedy and Comedy are both composed of *the same* letters," Aristotle remarks, in a critical exposition of the lettrist logic of ancient atomism.[30] In a theory of language and literature like Aristotle's, in which "spoken sounds are symbols of affections in the soul, and written marks are symbols of spoken sounds," this state of affairs is not the occasion for any confusion. Letters serve only to represent (and that at a second degree) original "affections in the soul," among which the comic and the tragic are clearly distinguishable.[31] But in the lettrist logic of the writing of the *Wake*, in which neither the soul and its affections nor language can be thought of as preceding the letters in which they're enfolded, the fact that tragedy and comedy are composed of the same letters really reveals something about the way the two genres are fundamentally mixed.

As it is posited in ancient atomism, the logical priority of letters does not imply this disturbance in the system of genres. In reducing literary appearances to the primary material of writing (via the systematic analogy that it draws between letters and atoms), atomism derives differences—like the difference between tragedy and comedy—from identities. Atoms are the solid units to which everything, in all its variety, can be reduced. Within atomism, to remark the sameness of the letters in tragedy and comedy is to notice solid building blocks. *Finnegans Wake* mirrors atomist lettrism in placing letters first, but the letters to which it gives priority are more like liquid than like the stuff of any building blocks. Identities dissolve in their movements, not into an undifferentiated primal stew or any other figure of origin, but always into something else.

Such a solvent cannot be a subject. Though the characters of alphabetic writing do have agency in the *Wake,* their agency is more like that of a household cleaning product than that of a human actor. They are no more the *Wake*'s underlying subject—what wakes throughout all the "hitherandthithering" of the figures that come and go—than any of its human characters are. Indeed, the meaning of "letter" in the *Wake* is as irreducibly multiple and un-atomic as the meaning of "wake." The different meanings of "letter" (the letters of the alphabet, the letters one sends in the mail, and "letters" as a metonymy for literature in general) are thoroughly compounded in the *Wake*'s "miscegenations and miscegenations." A letter, in the epistolarly sense, is rumored and awaited with great excitement throughout the book:

> The letter! The litter! And the soother the bitther! Of eyebrow pencilled, by lipstipple penned. Borrowing a word and begging the question and stealing tinder and slipping like soap. (93)

But the closer we get to the bottom of these rumors, the more overdetermined the sense of this "letter" becomes, compounding further the meanings of the word and rendering ever more abstract our picture of the rumored referent.

Chapter I.5 closely circles the problematic referent, advancing mock scholarly accounts and analyses of "the letter! The litter!" called for toward the end of chapter I.4. No reproduction of the letter is given, and both the comic opacity and the occasional lucidity of the critical glossing of the object give us plenty of reason to doubt that it could be. The status of the letter is problematic enough to have led to some debate in the mock secondary literature over whether the introduction of this letter into the world of letters alters the very meaning of "letter":

> No, assuredly, they are not justified, those gloompourers who grouse that letters have never been quite their old selves again since that weird weekday in bleak Janiveer (yet how palmy date in a waste's oasis!) when to the shock of both, Biddy Doran looked ad literature. (112)

This shocking and shocked literary figure—Biddy Doran—is one of the personae of "the original hen" (110), first seen "scratching" in the dump and discovering the letter in chapter I.1. Her name is given here as one of the many names of "Annah the Allmaziful . . . Bringer of Plurabilities," the maternal author-figure of the letter, her "untitled mamafesta" (104). The letter is now presented as the product of her "scratching" (111). Scavenger becomes author. And the more we learn about this author-hen and her technique of literary production, the more ambiguous her product becomes. The scratching by which a scrap of paper might be uncovered by a bird in a dump and the scratching by which marks are made on a page are not distinguishable in her not clearly literate literary activity. As a result, it is never clear that the original of the letter has ever, literally speaking, been written. Nor is it ever clear that, as a product of the hen's "scratching," the letter is merely a figure of speech.

And everything said about the letter in the very serious parody of scholarly commentary in chapter I.5 can be said for the whole of *Finnegans Wake,* from early remarks about the notable "nonpresence of inverted commas (sometimes called quotation marks)" (108), to later remarks on "the lubricitous conjugation of the last with the first: . . . the vocative lapse from which it begins and the accusative hole in which it ends itself" (122). Along the way, the mock scholarly reading of the letter offers odd object lessons (object lessons without the presentation of any clear object) in the reading of the *Wake*:

> Closer inspection of the *bordereau* would reveal a multiplicity of personalities inflicted on the documents or document and some prevision of virtual crime or crimes might be made by anyone unwary enough before any suitable occasion for it or them had so far managed to happen along. (107)

> The teatimestained terminal (say not the tag, mummer, or our show's a failure!) is a cosy little brown study all to oneself and, whether it be thumbprint, mademark or just poor trait of the artless, its importance in establishing the identities in the writer complexus (for if the hand was one, the minds of active and agitated were more than so) will be best appreciated by never forgetting that both before and after the battle of Boyne it was a habit not to sign letters always. Tip. (114–15)

Though the seriousness of scholarship is seriously satirized here in the infelicity of turns of phrase like "writer complexus," this characterization of the agency behind the writing of the letter tallies with some of Joyce's own characterizations of the agency at work in the writing of the *Wake.* Though obsessed with protecting his authorial rights, Joyce nonetheless liked to think that, even if "the hand was one" that wrote the *Wake,* "the minds of active and agitated were more than so."[32] "This book is being written by the people I have met or known," Joyce famously announced to Eugene Jolas.[33] And though one might, considering the source, be tempted to find some bad faith or at least false modesty in such a claim, the letter of which the *Wake* dreams in its every compounded word bears the mark of irreducible original multiplicity—the beauty mark of "Annah . . . Bringer of Plurabilities." In the early morning light at the very end of the *Wake,* a version of the much dreamed-of letter appears. The status of this text is entirely uncertain. No version of a document written in the hand (or birdfoot) of irreducible original multiplicity could ever be definitive. And, though a signature can always be forged, the final version of the letter is signed in this necessarily uncertain hand: "Pollabella" (beautiful hen), another name for Plurabelle, Anna Livia (615).

Joyce's grand claim that the *Wake* is written by many, not one, would be more dismissible than it turns out to be if this final version of the letter were delivered in such a way that we could at least say definitively where it ends—where the text of the plurally beautiful, beautifully plural hen ends and the writing of the rest of the *Wake* resumes. But the not necessarily literate scratching of Plurabelle doesn't stop at her signature.

Letter to the End of the Dream (The Address of the Wake*)*

This final version of the letter is usually thought of as beginning with "Dear. And we go on to Dirtdump. Reverend" (615) and ending, four pages later, with the six sentences—beginning with "P.S." and ending with "too"—that follow ALP's signature and salutation as "Alma Luvia, Pollabella" (619). According to this reading, the paragraph break before "Soft morning, city!" is taken to indicate the end of the postscript of the letter and the beginning of ALP's Molly Bloom–like "epilogue"/ "monologue," which ends with the last words of the book: "A way a lone a last a loved a long the" (628). But the ambiguity of this end of the "epilogue" complicates the question of where it begins (and the letter ends). The fadeout in which the "epilogue" ends is not final. The definite article with which the book ends belongs, by virtue of "a commodius vicus of recirculation," to the "riverrun" with which the book begins:

> riverrun, past Eve and Adam's, from swerve of shore to bend of bay, brings us by a commodius vicus of recirculation back to Howth Castle and Environs." (3)

In this curiously unapocalyptic reversal of first and last, the first words of the *Wake* turn out to be the completion of the last sentence of ALP's "epilogue." Her discourse has carried beyond the end of the book—beyond the outflow of Anna's Liffey into the salty sea of the largely bitter end of the book ("O bitter ending! . . . makes me seasilt saltsick and I rush, my only, into your arms" [627–28]).

In the deep waters of the ironic juncture of end and beginning in *Finnegans Wake,* any firm basis for saying that the paragraph break before "Soft morning, city!" signals the end of ALP's letter and the beginning of an "epilogue" dissolves.[34] The end of the book calls for a second reading of the beginning. On this second reading, the beginning of the book—"riverrun"—sounds like the beginning of the last version of the letter: "Dear. And we go on to Dirtdump. Reverend" (615). *Finnegans Wake*—a book about ending (*Finn*ing) again and again—begins in an echoing of the "Reverend" addressed in the opening of the last version of the letter.[35] "Echo, read ending!" (468) the *Wake* exclaims. Echoes echo only the endings of speech. In a text that begins in echoes—repeated ends—definitive ends disappear along with clean beginnings.

"Riverrun" echoes the "reverend" addressed in the final version of the *Wake*'s letter, but the ironic reverb produced in this "book of Doublends jined" (20) is such that "reverend" echoes "riverrun" too. The structural recursivity of the book baffles any attempt to say which comes first, and that baffling recursivity is reinscribed in every line. Take, again, the first line of the final version of the letter: "Dear. And we go on to Dirtdump. Reverend." Is "And we go on to Dirtdump" to be considered part of the letter itself? Or is it an editorial interpolation, part of a secondary literature in which the letter is embedded? If we take it to be part of the letter itself, how do we account for this departure from ordinary form, in which the letter would begin "Dear Reverend"? If we attribute this sentence instead to some commentator guiding us through the letter, how is "our" going "on to Dirtdump" on his or her authority to be clearly distinguished from the scratching in the dump by which the "original hen" finds the letter? And who or what is to be held responsible for the periods after "Dear" and "Reverend"?

Though "Dear" and "Reverend" would seem to be elements of an authentic letter, the mode in which they are presented to us is such that we cannot separate them, as pieces of directly reported speech, from the discourse of the commentary in which the report is given. As chapter I.5 avows in the form of a joke, the "non-presence of inverted commas (sometimes called quotation marks)" signals a boundless capability "of misappropriating the spoken words of others" (108). Without quotation marks setting the limits, the voice of commentary (the secondary literature) and the voice commented upon (the primary literature) flow together. They meet in the utterly ambiguous "we" of the first lines of the last version of the letter, which names, at once, the satirized learned community of commentators and readers that confers upon the scholar the right to his royal "we," the community of the author-commentator and the letter writer, the community of the letter writer and her addressee, and, in another ironic turn on the royal "we," the community unto herself of the feminine letter writer herself, who, as "Plurabelle," is already an irreducibly plural figure.

In Joycean grammar, this "we" is the slipperiest of words. Feminine, by virtue of its homophony with the "wee" of micturation, the symbol of which is the river (the Liffey, aka ALP), "we" also echoes, throughout the *Wake*, the French translation ("oui") of the famous feminine affirmation with which *Ulysses* ends. In the final version of the *Wake*'s letter, this "we" flows from "And we go on to dirtdump" into the ambiguous parenthesis of "May we add majesty?" and then on directly into what must be regarded as the body of the letter if the letter is to be regarded as having any body at all:

> Dear. And we go on to Dirtdump. Reverend. May we add majesty? Well, we have frankly enjoyed these secret workings of natures (thanks ever for it, we humbly pray) and, well, was really so denighted of this lights time. (615)

In the last words of the "body" of the letter (before the salutation that doubles as signature and the postscript, which I'm arguing has no identifiable last words), this "we" reappears in the grammatically singular form of a "wee one" who "woos" the "herewaker . . . young as of old" (619). This young replacement both is ("we are one") and isn't ALP. Modified by this "wee," "one" becomes plural.[36]

The postscript of the letter takes up the subject of this "wee one" in a less grammatically ambiguous third-person (i.e., "But she's still her deckhuman amber too" [619]). Because the letter itself stages this displacement of the first-person "we" in which it is written, the further shift to the first-person singular in what's often thought of as the beginning of ALP's "monologue"/"epilogue" ("Soft morning, city! Lsp! I am leafy speafing" [619]) is not entirely abrupt and thus does not alone justify talk of an "end of the letter." What's more, the action that this "I" of the "monologue/epilogue" narrates in the present tense—the flow of the feminine "we" of the letter out to sea as day breaks, sleepers begin to stir, and breakfast is made—is not separable from the action of the composition of ALP's letter. Because ALP "herself pits hen to paper" (615) and not pen, her letter is written through actions as seemingly unliterary as that of the making of breakfast, a matter of eggs ("eggburst, eggblend" [614]). The last word of the *Wake*—"the"—which Joyce, according to Louis Gillet, thought of as "the weakest word in the English language,"[37] gives a weak tea: *thé,* without the accent. We have heard rumors that the letter is marked by a "teastain" (111). Anna's henmanship is such that, searching for her letter, we are bound to search such marks for words and to see the mark of her rebus-like script in the *Wake*'s every last article.

On the tea-stained final page of the *Wake,* ALP, as the Liffey, as the voice of the book itself, says: "My leaves have drifted from me. All. But one clings to me still. I'll bear it on me. To remind me of. Lff! So soft this morning ours. Yes" (628). The Liffey "bears" this last leaf on her in the same way that she bears her letter in bearing her letter-carrying son, "Shaun the Post," downriver in chapter III.1. She is more than a conduit or a communicant, as the literature she bears comes from her in something like the same problematic sense in which her son comes from her. Both tenor and vehicle in the elusive metaphoricity of the writing of the last leaves of the *Wake,* the Liffey bears her leaf and inscribes it in one and the same flow. The time of inscription is the time of delivery. Writing is delivery. No letter composed in and under the terms of this metaphor could be delivered in full before the end of the book: "Lps. The keys to. Given! A way a lone a last a loved a long the" (628)

If the end of the letter were ever given in the *Wake,* it would have to be with the "giving away" of these last words—these keys. The letter is strongly associated with keys in the *Wake.* Not only is the letter generally treated as the "key" to the reading of the *Wake* as a whole (as we have seen in chapter I.5), but keys often come up in discussions of the letter. In chapter I.4, the letter is anxiously called for in the same breath in which a "kay" is sought:

> You and your gift of your gaft of your garbage abaht our Farvver! and gaingridando: Hon! Verg! Putor! Skam! Scham! Shames!
>
> And so it all ended. Artha kama dharma moksa. Ask Kavya for the kay. And so everybody heard their plaint and all listened to their plause. The letter! The litter! And the soother the bitther! (93)

The "kay" here is itself a letter, the first letter of the name of Kavya/Kate (ALP in the figure of an old crone). It is also the "key" necessary for any understanding of what has just been said ("Artha kama dharma moksa"). This desire for a key, which, as "kay," is already a letter in the alphabetical sense, leads to the anxious call for "the letter" in the epistolary sense. The letter is wanted as a key to the polyglot babble of this elusive "Shames" is wanted.

In the unlettered lettering of this babble, the "bitter" in "the soother the bitther" resonates (especially in its contiguity to "And so it all ended") with the "bitter ending" addressed so powerfully on the penultimate leaf of the *Wake.* The resonance between these calls (in want of a key) for a letter and the late apostrophe of the "bitter ending" is marked by the exclamation points that mark, throughout the *Wake*, the uncannily anxious tone of this plural voice. Both the apostrophe of the ending and the call for the letter are pitched (like the "Quoiquoiquoiquoiquoiquoi-quoiq!" of chapter I.8) as it were "on all sides,"[38] in the mode of an excitability that can't be channeled, in the final instance, into the form of any identifiable subject of excitations. Who calls for the letter in the end? (Which is to say, who is the subject of the desire for the "kay"?) Who doesn't? And to whom is the call addressed? And, in the final flow of "wee" to the sea at the end of the *Wake*, to what kind of subject can the hugely overdetermined pathos of "O bitter ending!" be attributed?

Throughout *Finnegans Wake*, the end is addressed, again and again ("Echo, read ending!"), in the bitterness of the want of a letter that can't come until it has been written and can't have been written before the end of the drama of the writing of the *Wake*, in all its subjectless excitability. "All the world's in want and is writing a letters" (278), say the children of ALP and HCE, in grammar much better than it may seem.[39] The desired end cannot be written within the present progress, punctuated by exclamations, of the writing of this universal want. *Finnegans Wake* ends not with "The End" but with a "the" without "end," which, as we've seen, brings us back to "the Reverend" ("the riverrun") of the beginning of the letter. The addressee of the letter, in its final but still incomplete version, is a prefixed "end," the prefix being "rever"—"to dream."

"You were dreamend, dear" (565) says the wife to her waking husband in chapter III.4, in a prefiguration (or an echo, on a second reading) of the "Dear . . . Reverend" of the opening address of the letter in its final version. And the "riverend name" (203) of the sinning Father Michael Arklow yokes "river-" and "rever-" to this same "end." The flow of the river toward the "bitter end" to which it addresses itself at the end of the *Wake* is thus mingled with the flow of dreaming in the *Wake*—a deep flow in the "rivering waters of, hitherandthithering waters of" the "Night!" called to or for (in another instance of an exclamation given without subject) at the end of the "Anna Livia Plurabelle" chapter (216). From "riverrun" on, the *Wake* is addressed to the end of the river of its dreaming.

The "keys" wanted in the desire that stirs all the wild excitement in the tone of the address of this end are "the keys of the seven doors of the dreamadoory in the house of the household of Hecech saysaith" (377). But, this house of HCE, as the house of "he, she, they saith," is the house of rumor—the rumored origin of all the rumors (often spread by "reverends," after confession)[40] that constitute the *Wake* from start to finish—and the house of rumor, like the house of sleep, has no doors in its doorways. Ovid's descriptions of these mythic structures remain authoritative:

> In the centre of the world, situated between earth and sky and sea, at the point where the three realms of the universe meet, is a place from which everything the world over can be seen, however far away, and to its listening ears comes every sound. There Rumour lives, in a home she has chosen for herself on a hilltop. Night and day the house lies open, for she has given it a thousand apertures and countless entrances, with never a door to barricade her thresholds. The whole structure is of echoing brass, and is full of noises, repeating words and giving back the sounds it hears.[41]

> Near the Cimmerian country is a cave, deeply recessed, a hollow mountain-side, the secret dwelling-place of languid Sleep . . . Voiceless quiet dwells there: but from the depths of the rocky cave flows the river of Lethe whose waters invite slumber as they glide, murmuring over whispering pebbles . . . There is not a door in the whole house, lest some turning hinge should creak.[42]

It might seem like keys are needed to the house of HCE in order to get to the bottom of all of the conflicting rumors about that central figure, but in fact the *Wake* is as bottomless as it is because the house belongs to rumors and dreams, and its "dreamadoory" is wide open from the start. Early on in the *Wake,* an open "Dor" is set in a place a lot like the place of the "end" that might have followed the final "the" of the book:

> So you need hardly spell me how every word will be bound over to carry three score and ten toptypsical reading throughout the book of Doublends Jined (may his forehead be darkened with mud who would sunder!) till Daleth, mahomahouma, who oped it closeth thereof the. Dor. (20)

In this "Dor" that appears only after a door that might close fails to appear before the full stop, the noun "Door" begins to become a verb: *Dors,* meaning "go to sleep" in the language that Joyce would have heard through the window as he was writing the *Wake.*[43] Anyone who has ever suffered a bout of insomnia knows that the door to sleep can slam shut, but this is not the "dor" that appears here. Behind the door that the wind of this or that night can slam shut lies sleep, the "dor" of which is always open to dreams.

The more "dor" opens beyond door in the *Wake*, the more rumors of a key or keys fly. The keys become the symbol of the openness of all channels in the *Wake*. They represent the object of all of the *Wake*'s rumoring, not because they might unlock a closed door behind which that object is kept, but because that object is more like keys than like a treasure hidden in a secret chamber to which we'd need keys. The end is in the means, which means that the means are useless. It doesn't mean, however, that they are meaningless. The recipient of the gift of keys that ALP makes in the final gesture of the *Wake* doesn't need to find a lock in which to use the keys in order for the gift to be meaningful. The gift is in the giving—in a giving away that itself opens "a way": "Lps. The keys to. Given! A way" (628). These keys could not be more overdetermined. They are at once the keys to "lps," "the keys to dreamland" (615), the keys to ALP's heart, and the keys to HCE's: "How you said how you'd give me the keys of me heart. And we'd be married till delth to uspart. And though dev do espart. O mine! Only, no, now it's me who's got to give" (626). Though the keys ALP gives are so heavily overdetermined as to go to practically everything, they are not master keys, the jailor's tool. Rather, they work only by a paradox of pure, autotelic seduction: if they have been given, then the seduction has already happened, and any door they promise to unlock has already been removed from its hinges.

It's common upon waking up to feel that a dream has left behind keys but has taken with it the addresses of the doors to which the keys correspond. A day spent trying to find those addresses is bound to be a melancholy one. HCE may be in for such a melancholy day. However, the reader of the *Wake* is not. The reader holds in his or her hands the address book that HCE—a character in the book—can only dream of. All of the addresses in the book are shared, making ALP's keys a pure gratuity, and making it possible for the reader to receive them guiltlessly, though the gift would seem to be addressed to HCE. The pleasure of reading the *Wake* is the pleasure of the pure gratuity of the "Quoiquoiquoiquoiquoiquoiquoiq!" with which it answers all demands for an explanation or a justification. The gratuitous life expressed in this exclamation belongs to no identifiable subject. It isn't the "real" life of this or that namable person, reachable at this or that particular address. In this sense, it is like a dream. But our enjoyment of it is all the more real as a result. Neither the vicarious (alienated) enjoyment we might take in the mastery of an author's star turn, nor the private enjoyment of the receipt of a letter addressed to any "me" or "you" in particular, the enjoyment of all of the excitement in the writing of the *Wake* cannot be felt without being shared. Exciting this enjoyment of a life that keeps no permanent address, the *Wake* addresses its reader, like its letter, to the bitterness of our common end, making, in the process, "lifework leaving" (12).

AFTERWORD

The Dream and Writing of Socrates

Since the day of Socrates' death, philosophy has been defined as a particular way of approaching death. Being philosophical has meant being philosophical about death. Waiting for sunset—the appointed hour of his death—Socrates discusses calmly what awaits him. No true philosopher, he says, should fear death, because philosophy pursues the separation of the soul from the body that death completes.[1] The true philosopher is already "nearly dead" (64b). And, indeed, Socrates shows no fear. From his quasi-suicidal apology up until the end, he shows himself ready to die. The death of Socrates is exemplary in its ease. As with any example, the real difficulty lies in following it. This is especially true for those of us who weren't there. For us, the example comes in the form of a second-hand tale, a kind of hearsay.

Even Socrates' best student receives the example this way. Plato is not present for Socrates' final hours. In the *Phaedo*—his account of these hours—Plato has Phaedo offer an excuse for him: "Plato, I believe, was ill" (59b). By allowing himself to be marked absent, Plato ironically implicates his text in the discussion that it represents. As Plato tells the tale, second-hand tales are the very material of Socrates' final discussion:

> Indeed, I too speak about this from hearsay, but I do not mind telling you what I have heard, for it is perhaps most appropriate for one who is about to depart yonder to tell and examine tales about what we believe the journey to be like. What else could one do in the time we have until sunset? (61e)

Socrates' inquiry into what happens to the soul in death can proceed only through the examination of second-hand accounts because no first-hand account of death is possible. He or she who dies doesn't live to tell the tale. As Wittgenstein puts it at the end of the *Tractatus*: "Death is not an event of life. Death is not lived through."[2] There is, of course, no shortage of second-hand accounts of death. In the irremediable absence of any verifying or falsifying first-hand account, rumors about death abound. In his last discussion, Socrates looks into these rumors without origin.

The very first rumor that Socrates examines in the *Phaedo* does not, on first glance, seem to be about any voyage in the land of the dead. It is a rumor about himself, and it comes to him in the form of a second-hand question. The rumor is that Socrates has been writing poems—versions of Aesop's fables and a Hymn to Apollo—and the question is why. Cebes asks Socrates the question on behalf of Evenus, who, like Plato, is not present among the discussants on Socrates' last day (60c, d). As it turns out, the rumor is true, giving the lie to the more widespread rumor, still alive today, that Socrates doesn't write. Socrates has, in fact, written poems during his stay of execution. (Socrates' execution is delayed until the return of an annual Athenian expedition to Delos, to honor Apollo.) He has written them, he says, in obedience to a recurring dream he used to have telling him to "make music" (60e).

Socrates had always thought he was obeying this dream in practicing philosophy, the highest form of music in his understanding.[3] However, in the dead time, or the extra life granted him until the return of the Athenian ship, Socrates tests whether it was not poetry that the dream had been calling him to. To an outsider like Evenus, this literary episode looks like a crisis in Socrates' sense of his philosophical vocation. But, as Socrates tells the tale, his lyrical turn to Aesop is material for a philosophical fable. He recounts his seemingly uncharacteristic explorations in writing as an exemplary story of philosophical openness to death. In answer to Evenus's question about his writing, Socrates gives an example to be followed. Socrates' response to Evenus, to be communicated to him by those present, is that he should, if he is wise, follow Socrates as soon as possible into death, the goal of all true philosophers (61b). When Evenus's friends express doubt that Evenus would want to do that, the discussion turns, until sunset, to Socrates' demonstration—via the examination of tales and hearsay—of all the reasons that he should.

When Evenus receives Socrates' response to his question about Socrates' writing, Socrates will no longer be alive. The rumor by which Socrates' answer will arrive to him is therefore like writing, in Socrates' understanding of what writing is. In the *Phaedrus*, Socrates famously defines writing in opposition to "living, breathing discourse."[4] Writing, unlike live speech, doesn't respond to questions:

> You know, Phaedrus, writing shares a strange feature with painting. The offsprings of painting stand there as if they are alive, but if anyone asks them anything, they remain most solemnly silent. The same is true of written words. You'd think they were speaking as if they had some understanding, but if you question anything that has been said because you want to learn more, it continues to signify just that very same thing forever . . . And when it is faulted and attacked unfairly, it always needs its father's support; alone, it can neither defend itself nor come to its own support.[5]

In the form in which it will arrive to Evenus, the example of Socrates' death will no longer be questionable. Socrates will no longer be there to answer questions about what he thinks he's doing in approaching death in this way. This renders the example both weaker and more absolute. Having been set, the impression of the example can only fade. It's as a living example of dying well that Socrates makes his impression. The dead, unquestionable example becomes a cult object—an ever more rigid model. The dying Socrates may live in the living memory of those who witnessed his death, but neither Evenus nor Plato can properly speak of "remembering" the scene of Socrates' death. The dying Socrates does not live in the rumor by which his example reaches Evenus and Plato, no matter how lively the rumor may be. Nor does he live in the writing by which it reaches us.

If Socrates had ever expressed even the hint of a belief that life might be sustainable in writing, then his last-minute experiment with literature would not seem like a departure for him. It's because his philosophy is so resolutely decided upon the deathly deficiency of writing as compared to live speech that his turn to writing at the end of his life raises the questions that it does, for Evenus and, indeed, for us. And if it did not seem like such a departure from philosophy, it would not make such a good philosophical story. The moral of the philosophical story is that death is not to be feared (Socrates' answer to Evenus's question is that Evenus should follow him gladly into death). As Socrates tells the tale, his openness to literature expresses his philosophical openness to death. His turn toward literature is an exercise in the philosophical departure from life.

So Socrates' tale of his last-minute literary experimentation is at once a tale of leaving and a tale of never having left. This double-sided story turns on the double sense of "death" in Socrates' discourse. The death he speaks of in pointing to the deadness of speech in writing is death as vacated life, a pale imitation of life. This death in writing—death as loss of the truth of presence—is not the true death the philosopher's heart desires. Less alive means less true in Socrates' theory of speech and writing. But in his theory of life—of philosophical life—less alive emphatically means more true. These two senses of death would seem to be contradictory, but in the dialectical witchcraft by which Socrates turns his departure from philosophy into philosophy, the more true and the less true are two sides of the same death. Death seen from the standpoint of life is less true than death seen with the eyes of the dead, which, up to the banks of Acheron, are covered by coins.[6]

From the standpoint of life, death is leaving. Death is defined negatively vis à vis life. But Socrates practices leaving life not because he doesn't want life, but because he positively desires something else. We can witness death as leaving more or less clearly depending upon how close we are to the live event. What we can't see live, under any circumstances, is what death looks like to the dead. It is this side of death that Socrates wants to see—that he strains to glimpse, through all his exemplary ease in leaving. He wants to see death with the eyes of the dead. He wants to see without seeing—to see what it looks like not to see. He can be questioned on his leaving, right up to the end, but he cannot be questioned on this. Socrates could corroborate or deny rumors about his leaving if he were here among us, but he could not corroborate or deny rumors about the other side of death even if he returned from the dead to respond to our questions, because whatever he might have seen of the other side of death he could have seen only in his own absence. Because he could not have been there as a subject for any of it, his tale of it would itself be a kind of rumor.

There is no practicing, in the present, for this absence to come. It comes without practice and all at once, whereas leaving takes a lifetime. But the only good reason to practice leaving life well is the desire to feel one's absence to come—to feel it already in the very impossibility of feeling it. If leaving well were the only aim of the exercise of leaving well, the exercise would be a show for the eyes of the living, not an expression of longing for the eyes of the dead. Such a ceremony might soothe the eyes of the living, mitigating the horror of death, but it wouldn't express a philosophical desire for death. And the practical, anesthetic function of the practice is not reliable enough to alone justify its rigors. In an early essay—"That to Philosophize is to Learn to Die"—Montaigne embraces the philosophical practice of dying well on the grounds that it improves life by lessening the horror of death. But later, in his essay "On Physiognomy," he finds that the practice cannot be defended on these practical grounds. Nature teaches us to die perfectly well, Montaigne decides. It's not worth thinking about constantly, and thinking about it may in fact make it worse.[7] When really put to the test by an honest practitioner like Montaigne, the practical grounds for the philosophical practice of dying well turn out to be unstable. Only an impractical desire for death can solidly justify the practice.

Desire for death is the only good reason to try to learn, through practice, to die well. But why, then, should anyone with this desire bother to practice philosophy at all? Why should the subject of this philosophical desire not simply kill himself or herself without delay? Socrates undertakes his examination of rumors of death in the *Phaedo* in response to a version of this question:

Then Cebes asked: "How do you mean Socrates, that it is not right to do oneself violence, and yet the philosopher will be willing to follow one who is dying?"

"Come now, Cebes . . . Have you not heard about such things?"

"Nothing definite, Socrates."

"Indeed, I too speak about this from hearsay, but I do not mind telling you what I have heard for it is perhaps most appropriate for one who is about to depart yonder to tell and examine tales about what we believe that journey to be like. What else could one do in the time we have until sunset?"[8]

The tales of the immortality of the soul that Socrates will tell and examine in the hours remaining to him are tales of the sweetness of death. They are meant to give some inkling of why it is that the philosopher wants death. They respond to that part of Cebes' question. They don't, however, seem to explain why the death-desiring philosopher shouldn't just kill himself or herself. The answer to this part of Cebes' question lies not in the tales but in the telling of them.

In his cheerful telling of these tales at the end of the day, Socrates demonstrates the calm in the face of death that makes his death exemplary. He also demonstrates, much less famously, a complete lack of control. Socrates answers Cebes' question about suicide through his simultaneous demonstration of these two seemingly contradictory attitudes toward death.

Even in the heights of his exemplary calm, Socrates never has his death at all under control, nor does he try to have it that way. The time of the death he awaits depends, literally, upon the winds:

> [The Athenians] have a law to keep the city pure while [the Athenian mission to Delos] lasts, and no execution may take place once the mission has begun until the ship has made its journey to Delos and returned to Athens, and this can sometimes take a long time, if the winds delay it . . . That is why Socrates was in prison a long time between his trial and his execution. (58b, c)

Socrates is glad to wait, not because he doesn't truly desire the death he awaits, but because the death he desires is the death you have to wait for. To kill himself would be to try to bring the timing of his death under his own control. Socrates resists all temptation to make such an attempt.

Though he holds the cup of poison in his own hands and downs it without delay, he does so only after the officer of the state tells him that the time for it has come (116c). While his impolitic apology is full of a death wish that verges upon the suicidal, and he firmly refuses to go into exile to escape his death sentence, he would not have taken the poison had he been pardoned at the last minute. His desire for death brings him right up to the line, but he never crosses it: he never tries to take the *time* of his death into his own hands.

The particular tranquility that Socrates demonstrates in the face of death rests upon maintaining philosophical desire for death right through to the end. Satisfaction of this desire is not in the philosopher's hands. The suicidal wish runs counter to the philosopher's desire for death. The suicidal subject seeks to control the coming of his or her death. Socrates—so near to suicide and yet so far—seeks to control himself so as not to attempt to control death. Though the tales Socrates tells of the immortality of the soul are calming, the desire he expresses in telling them in his final hours is a desire for death as disturbance. He longs not for more of the same calm, but for the source of the excitement hidden in the heart of that calm. He longs to know the real difference between life and death.

As near as Socratic philosophy may come to death in life, the practices by which it draws near to death also draw the clear, if fine, line between life and death. Approaching this line, Socrates approaches an essential difference. The calm in his approach is a way of containing the excitement that comes with desire for this difference—containing it so as to be able to sustain it. Though the disturbance that Socrates' desired death implies is not made explicit in the tales he tells and examines in the *Phaedo,* it is expressed in the act of the telling, and it arrives to us directly—direct descendants of Evenus that we are—in reading.

Evenus, Socrates' absent questioner with regard to writing, is the absent voice of this disturbance in the dialogue of Socrates' tranquil last day. He represents the voice of the city outside, for which Socrates' teaching of philosophical desire for death is an unpardonable disturbance of the peace, and for which his desired death, during the mission to Delos, would be an unacceptable stain. According to his friends, Evenus will not be so desirous of death as Socrates is (61c). If this rumor is to be believed, the question about Socrates' writing comes from a not entirely philosophical source. Evenus, bearer of the question of Socrates' writing, dreads death. And Socrates' gnomic response to Evenus's question about his writing—that Evenus should, if he's wise, follow him into death—is a provocation that hardly seems meant to calm his absent questioner. What calm Socrates communicates to the discussants present for his death is offset by Evenus's disturbance. Positioned, like Evenus, outside the inner circle that Socrates radiates in his presence on the threshold of his absence, the reader must share in Evenus's disquiet. The philosopher's calm inescapably implies the disturbance of the others outside the inner fold of the discussants present for Socrates' last "living, breathing discourse."[9] In philosophizing—in practicing this calm—Socrates was thus always guilty of a disturbance of the peace. In this sense, the city's condemnation of him to death is, though unjust, not entirely groundless.

The disturbance preserved in the heart of Socrates' exemplary calm is registered not in the "living, breathing" space of the dialogue but outside of it, among its readers—among the others who aren't there for Socrates' death.[10] Strangely, we others, Plato included, may therefore be closer to Socrates in death than were those present.[11] For, in dying, Socrates is absented from the scene of his death. And, in leaving the scene, he comes in to death as the outside toward which his deepest desire had been directed. His exemplary calm in leaving unfolds, upon arrival to the outside and to readers, into the disturbance that it had folded up inside itself in the "living, breathing" dialogue. This double movement (not a dialectic) of coming and going—of folding up and unfolding of the disturbance of death—is like the double movement of the dream in Freud's theory of it.

We've seen that the dream both serves sleep and refuses it in Freud's theory. To the "living, breathing" body of the sleeper, the dream is the very possibility of sleep and rest. But to the dreamer, who in entering the dream is absented from the sleepy scene of his or her "living, breathing" body, the dream is pure restlessness. In its role as "guardian of sleep," the dream wakes in the night, incorporating disturbances (from having to pee, to shouts from the apartment next door, to thoughts of one's own or another's death) into itself so as to maintain the sleeping body in sleep. Disturbance of sleep is the very stuff of dreams, the raw material of the waking figure of the guardian of sleep. Entering his or her dream, the dreamer leaves the sleepy bower scene of his or her body and comes into the other scene of all that threatens the sleep of that body. The irony of the situation—and this irony may underlie all Socratic irony, giving it its distinctive undertow—is that all sleep depends upon this departure of the dreamer into the sleeplessness of the dream. Sleep and rest depend upon the departure from sleep that the dream—the restless, guardian figure of disturbance—represents. But departure from one scene (the scene of sleep) is entry into another. From the standpoint of the bower scene of sleep, the dream represents the departure of the dreamer; meanwhile, from the standpoint of the other scene of the dream, the dreamer is an entering, not an exiting, figure.

According to this line of thinking about dreams, Socrates would be subject to the old dream that he reports in the *Phaedo* in something like the same irreducibly double way that he is subject to his death (on the one hand, as leaving, and, on the other, as coming in to his own absence). And this might begin to explain why Socrates, whose business it is to question everything, doesn't once question that the imperative he receives in his dream *must* be obeyed. Socrates' obligation to obey his dream would be like the unquestionable obligation to die. Certainly, these obligations go hand in hand in Socrates' interpretation of the imperative of his dream. On his interpretation, to fulfill one obligation is to prepare to fulfill the other. Obeying the dream means practicing for death—practicing philosophy—which means questioning everything but these fundamental obligations. But, curiously, the fulfillment of his obligation to die cannot mean the end of his obligation to his dream if his interpretation of his dream is correct. The questioning that he is called to by his dream is a way of becoming as nearly dead as possible. And where questioning is a way of being ever more dead, death can mean only yet more thoroughgoing questioning. This restless death is much more like a dream than it is like the sleep that a dream assures.

This likeness of the philosopher's death to a dream might seem to indicate that the philosopher is really just dreaming of a continuation of philosophical life through all of his big talk of desire for death. But the process of questioning through which Socrates approaches death is endless not because death is not an end to life but because the end of life is the origin, not the end, of the philosopher's questions. It is the source of the unrest from which questions come, the stuff of the dream that first calls him to a life of questioning. In the death that he calmly approaches, Socrates cannot be at rest. Leaving life, Socrates leaves the "living, breathing" space of the dialogue and enters a space for questioning lying outside the limits of dialogue. He cannot respond to our questions here. If he could, his questioning could come to an end. He could report authoritatively on his own death, and we'd have no need for Plato's writing. It's from this space outside—as in a dream from which, because it assures no sleep, one will not wake—that Socrates continues to pose his questions to us.

NOTES

Where two page references are separated by a slash, the first reference is to the English translation of the work in question and the second is to the original.

INTRODUCTION: THE OTHER NIGHT

1. See, for example, *The Space of Literature,* 163–76/213–32.

2. The October 27, 2005 edition (No. 7063) of *Nature* magazine gives an overview of the field of sleep studies. J. Allen Hobson's article contains good notes on the role of new medical imaging technologies in the "observation" of dreaming.

3. See, for example, *The Space of Literature,* 171/226.

4. Chapter 22 of the Second Part of *Don Quixote* "recounts the great adventure of the Cave of Montesinos that lies in the heart of La Mancha [*el corazón de la Mancha*]" (597/694).

5. Herman Braet argues that this figure represents a conception of dreaming derived from the *Song of Songs.* See his "Rêve, réalité, écriture," 21.

6. "Farai un vers de dreyt nien / . . . Qu'enans fo trobatz en durmen / Sus un chivau" is the original, in Bond's edition of *The Poetry of William VII, Count of Poitiers, IX Duke of Aquitaine,* 14.

7. See again page 597 in the English, 694 in the Spanish.

8. For the purposes of psychoanalytic interpretation, "whatever the dreamer tells us must count as his dream, without regard to what he may have forgotten or altered in recalling it" (Freud, *Introductory Lectures on Psychoanalysis,* 85).

9. "What am I then? Thou spakest of my tribe: / What tribe?"—The tall shade veiled in drooping white / Then spake [. . .] "Art thou not of the dreamer tribe? / The poet and the dreamer are distinct, / Diverse, sheer opposite, antipodes. / The one pours out a balm upon the world,/ The other vexes it" (lines 193–202).

10. Lautréamont calls, famously, for an unthinkable democracy in literature: "La poésie doit être faite par tous. Non par un. Pauvre Hugo! Pauvre Racine! Pauvre Coppée! Pauvre Corneille! Pauvre Boileau! Pauvre Scarron! Tics, tics, et tics" ("Poésies," 255).

11. At the center of *The Space of Literature* there's a chapter called "Inspiration." In a note at the beginning of the book, Blanchot directs the reader to the central section of this chapter: "A book, even a fragmentary one, has a center which attracts it. This center is not fixed, but is displaced by the pressure of the book. . . . He who writes the book writes it out of desire for this center and out of ignorance. The feeling of having touched it can very well be only the illusion of having reached it. When the book in question is one whose purpose is to elucidate, there is a kind of methodological good faith in stating toward what point it seems to be directed: here, toward the pages entitled "Orpheus's Gaze [*Le Regard d'Orphée*]."

12. Freud, *The Interpretation of Dreams*, 312.

13. The last words of George Eliot's *Middlemarch.*

14. See Empson, *Some Versions of Pastoral*, 4–5; and Guillory, *Cultural Capital*, 85–133.

15. See Johnson, *The Feminist Difference*, 129–153.

16. Milton, *Lycidas*, line 186.

17. As García Lorca puts it in *Asi que pasen cinco años*: "Nadie puede abrir semillas / en el corazon del sueño [no one can make anything grow in the heart of the dream]" (III.i.3–4).

18. The last of these, Benjamin's unfinished *Arcades Project*, speaks the dying words of the age in its call "to read what was never written" in the iron and glass of the big dream of the modern city (416).

19. Beckett, *Molloy*, 138/188

20. "you must go on, I can't go on, I'll go on" (Beckett, *The Unnamable*, 414/213).

21. Beckett, *The Unnamable*, 301/24.

THE DREAM AS WRITING: FREUD'S THEORY

1. Freud, *Introductory Lectures on Psychoanalysis*, 85.

2. Freud, *New Introductory Lectures on Psychoanalysis*, 10.

3. Freud, *A Metapsychological Supplement to the Theory of Dreams*, 228.

4. Thus Freud will sometimes speak of the "language of the dream thoughts" (*The Interpretation of Dreams*, 312).

5. Freud, *The Interpretation of Dreams*, 312

6. Ibid.

7. Ibid. Though Freud considers the dream to be a pictographic script, he often appeals to scripts more familiar to his readers in illustrating his central claim that the combinatory principles at work in the dream are graphematic:

> Whenever they [dreams] show us two elements close together, this guarantees that there is some specially intimate connection between them among the dream-thoughts. In the same way, in our system of writing *ab* means that the two letters are to be pronounced in a single syllable. If a gap is left between the *a* and the *b*, it means that the *a* is the last letter of one word and the *b* is the first of the next one. (*Interpretation of Dreams*, 349)

> Two thoughts which occur in immediate sequence without any apparent connection are in fact part of a single unity which has to be discovered; in just the same way, if I write an *a* and a *b* in succession, they have to be pronounced as a single syllable *ab*. The same is true of dreams. (*Interpretation of Dreams*, 280)

Freud has further recourse to this explanation by means of the *a*'s and *b*'s of alphabetic writing in his case history of "Dora" (71).

8. Freud, *Some Additional Notes on Dream-Interpretation as a Whole*, 131.
9. Freud, *The Claims of Psycho-Analysis to Scientific Interest*, 177.
10. Freud, *The Interpretation of Dreams*, 647.
11. Freud, *The Claims of Psycho-Analysis to Scientific Interest*, 177.
12. Derrida, "Freud and the Scene of Writing," 220.
13. Derrida, *Of Grammatology*, 15.
14. Derrida, "Freud and the Scene of Writing," 209.
15. Gasché, *The Tain of the Mirror*, 274.
16. Derrida, "Freud and the Scene of Writing," 209.
17. Derrida, "Signature, Event, Context," 318.
18. Freud, *Jokes and Their Relation to the Unconscious*, 167. Freud avoids metaphysical terminology for naming absence in calling, here, upon "*Absenz*," which can be used in a medical sense to name episodes, like epilectic fits, in which the subject of the episode is not quite there.
19. Freud, *The Interpretation of Dreams*, 216.
20. Ibid., 339.
21. Ibid., 454.
22. Ibid., 330.
23. Wittgenstein, *Tractatus Logico-Philosophicus*, 6.4311.
24. Malcolm, "Dreaming and Skepticism," 116. This article summarizes Malcolm's argument in his book called *Dreaming*.
25. Malcolm, "Dreaming and Skepticism," 120.
26. Ibid., 121.
27. Ibid., 119.
28. Freud, *The Interpretation of Dreams*, 555–56.
29. Ibid., 313.
30. See, for example, the *New Introductory Lectures*:

> We have to transform the manifest dream into the latent one, and to explain how, in the dreamer's mind, the latter has become the former. The first portion

> is a *practical* task, for which dream-interpretation is responsible. The second portion is a *theoretical* task, whose business it is to explain the hypothetical dream-work; and it can only be a theory. (9)

> This is what I wanted to say to you, Ladies and Gentlemen, about dream-interpretation, whose task it is to lead the way from the manifest dream to the latent dream-thoughts. When this has been achieved, interest in the dream, so far as practical analysis is concerned, is for the most part at an end. We add the communication we have received in the form of the dream to the rest of the patient's communications and proceed with the analysis. (16)

31. Freud, *The Interpretation of Dreams*, 545.

32. Freud, *Jokes*, 159.

33. The "preconscious" corresponds to a pre-Freudian, merely privative determination of the unconscious. Freud distinguishes his new conception of the "unconscious" from the traditional privative conception:

> It is not without intention that I speak of "our" unconscious. For what I thus describe is not the same as the unconscious of the philosophers or even the unconscious of Lipps. By them the term is used merely to indicate a contrast with the conscious . . . The new discovery that we have been taught by the analysis of psychopathological structures and of the first member of that class—the dream—lies in the fact that the unconscious (that is, the psychical) is found as a function of two separate systems, and that this is the case in normal as well as in pathological life. Thus there are two kinds of unconscious, which have not yet been distinguished by psychologists. Both of them are unconscious in the sense used by psychology; but in our sense one of them, which we term the *Ucs.*, is also *inadmissible to consciousness*, while we term the other the *Pcs.* because its excitations . . . are able to reach consciousness. (*Interpretation of Dreams*, 652)

Freud repeats these thoughts five years later in his book on jokes (162).

34. Freud, *The Interpretation of Dreams*, 600.

35. Freud, *Remarks on the Theory and Practice of Dream Interpretation*, 111. Freud introduces this distinction in 1923 in order to clarify the seeming contradictions, in the earlier theory, between claims that the instigation of the dream is always to be found in the thought processes of the dream-day and claims that the unconscious, in which there's neither night nor day, begins the dream by seizing upon straggling daytime thoughts. Though it may not require any "modification in the theory of dreams," the distinction does loosen up more than a few of the claims of the earlier theory. For example, in light of the distinction, Freud does admit that, in some cases, "one dream leads off from another, taking as its central point some element which was lightly touched upon in its predecessor, and so on," though it remains the case that, "we find more frequently that dreams are not attached to one another but are interpolated into a successive

series of portions of waking thought" (111). In the earlier theory, such an admission would not have been possible, as Freud's main drive in the beginning was to prove that dreams could, contrary to the usual opinion at the time, be interpolated, day by day, into the stream of waking thought—that "every dream reveals itself as a psychical structure which has a meaning and which can be inserted at an assignable point in the mental activities of waking life" (*Interpretation of Dreams,* 35). This loosening-up of the earlier theory didn't, however, extend to Freud's dealings with Breton, whose interest in dreaming as the main stream in thinking, more truly continuous than the lesser reality of the day to day, was completely unacceptable to Freud. But while Freud, no surrealist, would never regard dreaming as the main stream of thinking, he does, here in later life, admit the possibility of streams of dreaming connecting night to night and not day to day.

36. Freud, *The Interpretation of Dreams,* 545. Jean-François Lyotard looks deep into this claim in an essay called, straightforwardly, "The Dream-Work Does Not Think." Lyotard would not agree that the transforming work of the dream, which he opposes to the discourse of the dream, is the work of a kind of writing. Writing remains, along with language, thought, and law, on the side of discourse in his conceptual scheme. "The space of writing" is the space of language in Lyotard's account—a two-dimensional space (22). The dream-work crumples this space, opening up a dimension of depth of sense beyond the limits of law and language (23). According to Lyotard's scheme, transcription into writing doesn't count as transformative work on discourse. A transcription, for him, is merely another "discourse based on a discourse." In order to come to this conclusion, Lyotard has to avoid most of what Freud actually says about writing and transcription in chapter 6 of the dreambook and elsewhere. In the dream-work of his own essay, Lyotard clumps language, writing, and thought too tightly together and thus misses the subtle, internal differences that Freud's theory plays with.

37. Freud, *The Interpretation of Dreams,* 385.

38. Ibid., 509. According to Freud, the extraordinary speed of the dream with respect to daytime speech and thought would not be conceivable if the dream-work had to invent anything for itself. In his 1878 treatise on *Le sommeil et les rêves,* Maury recounts a very elaborate dream that had to have been dreamt in nothing more than a moment. Says Freud:

> We should never dare to attribute such rapidity to thought-activity in waking life, and we should therefore be driven to conclude that the dream-work possesses the advantage of accelerating thought to a remarkable degree . . . I myself would propose the following explanation of this dream. Is it so highly improbable that Maury's dream represents a phantasy which had been stored up ready-made in his memory for many years and which was aroused—or I would

rather say "alluded to"—at the moment at which he became aware of the stimulus which woke him? If this were so, we should have escaped the whole difficulty of understanding how such a long story with all its details could have been composed in the extremely short period of time which was at the dreamer's disposal—for the story would have been composed already. (*Interpretation of Dreams*, 534)

39. Freud, *Remarks*, 114.
40. Freud, *Some Notes*, 113.
41. Ibid., 133–34.
42. Ibid., 132–33.
43. Freud, *The Interpretation of Dreams*, 267. Freud's emphasis.
44. Freud, *An Outline of Psychoanalysis*, 171.
45. Freud, *Metapsychological Supplement*, 225.
46. Ibid., 225.
47. Ibid., 226.
48. See, for example, *Jokes*, 171 and *Outline*, 166.
49. Freud, *The Interpretation of Dreams*, 143.
50. Ibid., 564.
51. *Numquam minus solum esse quam cum solus esset* (quoted in Arendt, *The Human Condition*, 325).

DREAM AND WRITING IN BLANCHOT

1. These examples are from *The Space of Literature*, 38, 108/37, 135, translation modified; *The Book to Come*, 11/19; and *Lautréamont and Sade*, 43/243.

2. Reflecting upon the surrealist "experience," the lessons of which he takes great pains to learn throughout his critical writing, Blanchot admires most its radically reflexive form: "The surrealist experience is the experience of experience . . . In works such as these thought is experience inasmuch as the written comes to thought in the movement of writing. Knowledge does not exist before writing" (*The Infinite Conversation*, 421/618). In this "experience of experience," "experience" cannot be imagined to preexist writing but is, from the beginning, experience of writing.

3. Blanchot, *The Space of Literature*, 33/31. Translation modified. The original is "Écrire . . . c'est passer du Je au Il, de sorte que ce qui m'arrive n'arrive a personne." Throughout this chapter, I will modify the published translations where needed in order to leave Blanchot's *Il* untranslated. Blanchot sometimes capitalizes his *Il* and sometimes leaves it in lower case. I will follow him back and forth here. But, in either case, it's the same *il*.

4. Blanchot, *The Infinite Conversation*, 380/558.

5. *The Infinite Conversation*, 384/563. Translation modified.

6. Though what speaks in writing is not, for Blanchot, any more a collectivity than it is an individual subject, Blanchot does, throughout his post-May 1968 writings—and especially in *The Unavowable Community*—insistently affirm an impossible "community" beyond and before any concept of unity. Much of this affirmation passes by way of the central theme of friendship in his writings, the relationship between friends being, for Blanchot, irreducible to any one-to-one correspondence of one to an other conceived of as *another one*. The relationship—the *partage*—is not intersubjective and not an exchange; it has, rather, the form of an *entretien* in which each *entretenant* finds himself or herself always already "implicated in a speech [*une parole*] that is exterior to him" (*The Infinite Conversation*, xix/xix). This is a shared implication in what Blanchot calls, on the title page of the first section of *The Infinite Conversation*, the "speech of writing," "Plural Speech."

7. Blanchot, *The Infinite Conversation*, 385/564–65.

8. Ibid., 47/67.

9. Ibid., 46/66.

10. The reflection that Blanchot sustains, throughout his work, on "impossibility" grows out of Heidegger's thinking of death as the "possibility of the absolute impossiblity of *Dasein*" (*Being and Time*, 294/250, 299/255, 307/262, 378/329). Blanchot tries, with Heidegger and against Heidegger, to think of the undeniable coming-to-pass of death not as an indication that the impossible is somehow possible, but as pure impossiblity—impossibility that comes to pass *as impossibility*. For Blanchot, though death happens, it is in no way in our power; it is not something that any subject can be said to do or to be capable of doing, even in the case of suicide.

11. Blanchot, "Dreaming, Writing," 141–42/164.

12. Blanchot returns to this passage nine years later in *The Writing of the Disaster* citing it prominently there, and analyzing it in the context of a reflection on the "désastre" as "veille" (59/97).

13. Insomnia is an obsession for Blanchot. He shares this life-long obsession with his friend Levinas, who begins to elaborate a line of thinking on it in *Existence and Existents*, in which he distinguishes between "attention," which is directed toward objects, and "vigilance," which is "absorbed in the rustling of unavoidable being" and "anonymous" (65/110). In its irreducibility to a namable subject of consciousness, this "vigilance" shakes up the phenomenological terminology within which Levinas is working:

> Our affirmation of an anonymous vigilance goes beyond the *phenomenon*, which already presupposes an ego, and thus eludes descriptive phenomenology. Here description would make use of terms while striving to go beyond their consistency; it stages *personages*, while the *there is* [the *il y a*, the elemental state of affairs in which insomniac vigilance is absorbed] is the dissipation of personages. A method is called for such that thought is invited to go beyond intuition. (66/112)

Blanchot, like Levinas, takes up this invitation throughout his thinking. For both Levinas and Blanchot, this "vigilance" precedes the distribution of subjects and objects and thus cannot be attributed to any definite subject. "Cela," or "il," or "le neutre" *veille.* However, unlike Blanchot, Levinas does not link the vigilance of insomnia to the dream. For Levinas, the dream "encases itself in sleep" (66/110), and Levinas, like Blanchot, defines "sleep" as the placement—the positioning par excellance—of a subject of consciousness.

14. Blanchot, *The Space of Literature,* unnumbered prefatory page/9.

15. See, for example, "Dreaming, Writing," 147/169.

16. I explore both of these distinctions at greater length toward the end of this chapter.

17. See, for Blanchot's use of "duplicité," *L'Entretien infini,* 42: "L'image est la duplicité de la révélation. Ce qui voile en révélant, le voile qui révèle en revoilant dans l'indécision ambigue du mot révéler, c'est l'image. L'image est image en cette duplicité, non pas le double de l'object, mais le dédoublement initial qui permet ensuite à la chose d'être figurée . . . c'est . . . le tour du tournant . . . La parole dont nous essayons de parler est retour à cette première tournure." Or, *L'Amitié,* 186, where Blanchot finds, in the heart of the monism of Jean Paulhan, "la duplicité irréductible de l'Un." In *L'Espace littéraire,* Blanchot exposes this *duplicité,* as in *L'Entretien infini,* with respect to the image: "l'image . . . risque aussi constamment de nous renvoyer, non plus à la chose absente, mais à l'absence comme présence, au double neutre de l'object en qui l'appartenance au monde s'est dissipée: cette duplicité n'est pas telle qu'on puisse la pacifier par un ou bien ou bien capable d'autoriser un choix et d'ôter du choix l'ambiguité qui le rend possible. Cette duplicité renvoie elle-même à un double sens toujours plus initial" (353).

18. The French is "Le piège de l'*autre* nuit, c'est la première nuit où l'on peut pénétrer." It's not entirely clear whether the first night is itself the other night's trap, or whether we stumble into the other night's trap as we make our way through the first night. But, either way, the other night catches us sleeping.

19. Blanchot attacks traditional ideas of literary power and glory as outdated at the end of *The Book to Come*:

> The extraordinary turmoil that causes the writer to publish before writing, that causes the public to form and transmit what it does not understand, the critic to judge and define what he does not read, and the reader, finally, to have read what is not yet written—this movement that confuses, by anticipating them each time, all the various moments of the work's formation, also gathers them together in the search for a new unity. Thus the richness and poverty, the pride and humility, the extreme disclosure and the extreme solitude of our literary work, which has at least the merit of desiring neither power, nor glory. (250/340)

The old desire for power and glory through literature is part of a desire for eternity. In this desire, the nostalgia for which Blanchot sees in the decadence all around him, literature is a link to the eternal:

> Speech that is eternalized in written work promises some immortality. The writer joins forces with what triumphs over death; he ignores the temporary; he is the friend of the soul, man of the spirit, guarantee of the eternal. Many critics, even today, seem sincerely to believe that the vocation of art and literature is to eternalize man. (245/333, translation modified)

In 1980, more than 20 years later, Blanchot is still locked in tooth and nail battle with this persistent nostalgia. The last sentence of *The Writing of the Disaster* (two italicized fragments in something like the form of writing-notes, notes for future writing, follow it) is a cry for help in this battle: "Let us share eternity, so as to render it transitory" (220, my translation).

20. Many of Blanchot's thoughts on the dream and the night vis à vis the experience of writing are thoughts on Mallarmé. The allusion here is to *Igitur,* a central instance of Mallarmé's "rêve pur d'un Minuit . . . où doivent être jetés les dés."

21. See, for example, 172/226.

22. Wahl, *1848–1948: Cent années de l'histoire de l'idée d'éxistence,* 20. My translation.

23. Ibid.

24. Montaigne, "Of Repentance," 610–11. Translation slightly modified.

25. Deleuze, *Difference and Repetition,* 23/36.

26. Ibid., 10/18.

27. Aristotle, *On Dreams,* 730 (459a1).

28. Blanchot, *The Space of Literature,* 264–65/357–58.

29. Ibid., 265/358–59.

30. Ibid., 264/357.

31. Ibid., 266–67/361.

32. Ibid., 267/361.

33. Though Blanchot, sharing a fascination widespread in his generation, reflects often on this stucture, he never names it *mise en abîme,* the going term for it since Gide in France (for a good genealogy and exploration of the uses of this strange term from medieval heraldry, see Dällenbach, *Le récit spéculaire*). He tends, rather, to redescribe it, in every instance, from scratch. His sense of his own implication in the structure, wherever he encounters it, makes it impossible for him to speak from outside of it, in the structuralist, as it were scientific, nomenclature. He tends to speak of what many of his contemporaries would call *mise en abîme* from the inside, as an existential predicament—as the very structure of the basic fact of being, from the start, "implicated in a speech [*une*

parole] that is exterior to him" (*The Infinite Conversation*, xix/xix), or implicated, impossibly, in the experience of writing. Derrida, in his studies of this basic structure in Blanchot's fictions, also avoids the term, speaking instead of a "double chiastic invagination of the edges [*double invagination chiasmatique des bords*]" (*Parages* 244, 270–72). This way of speaking has the advantage of de-dramatizing the situation of being without clear exit from a fiction. No grand abysses here, just the turning of things inside out and back again in such a way that the source of the fiction cannot be safely located outside of it and, in turn, the inside of the fiction becomes an "outside." This fundamental structure of fiction is often described by analogy to the mirror, and, as a result, the widespread fascination with this structure through the 1970's has since been derided as a "narcissistic" turning away of Literature, with a capital L, from everything that isn't Literature (i.e., its "contexts" or "histories"). But, in Blanchot's conception of the inside outs and outside ins of literature, what Derrida will call "une double invagination chiasmatique des bords" is the very structure of the utter impossibility of any such turning away—an impossibilty that defines any literature worth the name. If there's any turning away in Blanchot, it is turning away from the work, with all of its clever structures, and towards the ruin, represented by Eurydice, of all of those structures—towards what he calls "the outside." By this inside out and back again structure in Blanchot, "literature" names an irreducible relation with the outside, the impossibility of withdrawal to any solipsistic inside.

34. Blanchot, *The Space of Literature*, 31/28.

35. Ibid., 268/362. In Blanchot, the unconditioned—everything he marks with the adjective "pure" ("pure movement," "pure resemblance")—remains sovereign, though denuded of power and glory. What's characterized as pure still "reigns," impossibly, in this exile. Throughout his late work, Derrida, following through on the gesture that Blanchot begins in stripping the unconditioned of power and glory, tries to remove the unconditioned from its traditional association with sovereignty.

36. Ibid.

37. This region without resting place is like the desert:

> When speech becomes prophetic, it is not the future that is given, it is the present that is taken away, and with it any possibility of a firm, stable, lasting presence. Even the Eternal City and the indestructible Temple are all of a sudden—unbelievably—destroyed. It is once again like the desert, and speech is also desert-like, this voice that needs the desert to cry out and that endlessly awakens in us the terror, understanding, and memory of the desert . . . Prophetic speech is a wandering speech that returns to the original demand of movement by opposing all stillness, all settling, any taking root that would be rest. (*The Book to Come*, 79/110)

38. "The Two Versions of the Imaginary" is the title of the appendix in which this distinction is worked out (*The Space of Literature,* 254–63/341–55).

39. Blanchot explores, throughout his work, what he calls, in *The Space of Literature,* "double death [*la double mort*]" (103/129). The broad strokes in my summary here are thus both unjust and necessary. Pages 87–107/105–34 of *The Space of Literature* are the closest Blanchot comes to a summary.

40. Again: "To write," for Blanchot, "is to pass from *Je* to *Il,* such that what happens to me happens to no one" (*The Space of Literature,* 33/31, translation modified).

41. Shakespeare, *Richard III,* I.iv, 42–45.

42. Blanchot, *L'Ecriture du désastre,* 49. All translations from this text are mine.

BECKETT'S RESTLESSNESS

1. Beckett, *Molloy,* 66/88.

2. Beckett, *The Unnamable,* 301/24. As the trilogy proceeds, the conditions in which the characters find themselves become more and more unfavorable to writing (considered in its "manual aspect"). Unlike the unnamable narrator of the last book of the trilogy, Malone can, though bedridden, lift his hand from his knee. But he has issues with his implements. He has only a single pencil (another may be lost somewhere in the bed) and a single notebook. These scanty writing supplies are not only exhaustible (in much the same way that Malone's life is exhaustible) but they are also subject to loss. Indeed, his hold on these minima of the "manual aspect" of writing is not firm, and, in the looseness of that hold, some of the stranger aspects of his writing come into view. For example, it's not clear how he manages to narrate, in the present tense, the loss of his notebook: "I fear I must have fallen asleep again. In vain I grope, I cannot find my exercise-book. But I still have the pencil in my hand. I shall have to wait for day to break. God knows what I am going to do till then" (*Malone Dies,* 208/57). He can't have written these sentences without his notebook, and yet they are written in the present. In this gap in the logic of the proposition that the text we are reading is the text that Malone is writing (a proposition reasserted in the later episode of the loss of his pencil, which is represented by an abrupt break in the text [222/79]), we can certainly see the hand of a less fictional author at work. Beckett shows his hand in his scenes of writing without hands. However, he never offers his hand as a resolution of the enigma that the scenes lay out. On the contrary, the more he shows his hand, the more seriously we are bound to take his stories of the irreducibility of writing to its "manual aspect."

3. Beckett, *Molloy,* 41/54. Hugh Kenner sees Beckett's fiction as "less close to any other reality than to the mental world of a man sitting in a room before a sheaf of papers" ("Man in the Room," 77). I will try to show in this chapter

that, though Beckett's fiction is, as Kenner indicates, centrally concerned with writing (and not with "other realities" imagined to preexist or to otherwise exist outside of writing), the existence of the "man in the room" cannot be thought of as a point in reality to which the fiction might ultimately be referred.

4. Beckett, *The Unnamable*, 299/21.

5. Beckett, *Molloy*, 78/105.

6. Beckett, *The Unnamable*, 414/213. The unnamable speaker says that it "would surprise" him to find himself on the threshold of the silence that he's been seeking, but in the same breath he suggests that his knowledge that he'll never know exactly where he stands places him, at the end, "in the silence." He has said some lines earlier that he would be similarly "surprised" if he were dreaming:

> I don't know, perhaps it's a dream, all a dream, that would surprise me, I'll wake, in the silence, and never sleep again, it will be I, or dream, dream again, dream of a silence, a dream of silence, a dream silence, full of murmurs, I don't know, that's all words, never wake, all words, there's nothing else, you must go on, that's all I know. (414/212)

Silence might be the end of such a dream, or such a dream might be a dream of silence, or the silence of which he's speaking might be that of such a dream—"that's all words." The silence of his dreams—the silence about which he can't stop talking—is not the kind one can hold, in knowledge or otherwise. Rather, he's *in* this silence or out of it, and, if he's in it, he's in no position to judge where he stands. It's the real impossibility of knowing, from within, whether or not he's already in it that makes his task impossible and his situation comical. Though he is joking a little when he says, in the very last lines of the book, that he can't know whether or not he's in the silence because "in the silence you don't know," the speaker isn't lying. The silence of the unnamable speaker's dreams is not a quiet knowable by opposition to speech but the unknowable silence in the heart of speech, which beats on beyond his power.

7. Beckett, *Le monde et le pantalon*, 44. All translations from this text are mine.

8. Samuel Beckett, *Three Dialogues*, 103/14.

9. Ibid., 112, 125/20, 30.

10. Ibid., 119–20/24.

11. Beckett, *Peintres de l'empêchement*, 58. All translations from this text are mine.

12. Ibid., 54. The inscrutability of the obligation is made clear in *Three Dialogues*. Asked why the painter is obligated to paint if "there is nothing to paint and nothing to paint with," Beckett answers: "I don't know" (119/24).

13. See again Beckett, *The Unnamable*, 301/24.

14. Ibid., 342/93.

15. Beckett, *Le Monde et le pantalon*, 35.

16. As in, "It's not for me to judge. What would I judge with?" (351/108). Or, "Go mad, yes, but there it is, what would I go mad with" (383/161). In this second example, the rhetorical question is added in the English. There are other examples where the question appears in the French and disappears in the English, such as the following: "Le dernier pas. Avec quoi?" (78 in the French, 333 in the English).

17. Writing without hands would make a good miracle.

18. Dante, *Purgatorio* (iv, 97–135).

19. *Purgatorio* is Dante's dreambook. Despite the strong influence of Macrobius and the tradition of the *Somnium Scipionis*/Vision of Er on the grand flights of *Paradiso*, *Purgatorio* is, of the three books of the *Divine Comedy*, the one most devoted to episodes and questions of sleeping and dreaming. In picking such a plain figure as Belacqua out from *Purgatorio*, Beckett is not rejecting the great book's dreaminess. Rather, he is looking into the foul rag and bone shop of its waking heart—the non-industrious yet restless scene of its production.

20. Beckett never accepted the label of "absurdist" often attached to his works. In *The Unnamable*, he points to a distinction between "the impossible," which he embraces, and "the absurd":

> That the impossible should be asked of me, good, what else could be asked of me? But the absurd! (338/85)

21. See Beckett, *Quad et autres pièces pour la télévision*, 50–54.

22. Beckett, *The Unnamable*, 383/161.

23. See chapter 2.

24. Beckett, *Molloy*, 92/125.

25. See also page 96/131: "Or was it in order to win a few more moments of peace that I instinctively avoided giving my mind to it?"

26. He has, handy in his desk drawer, a tube of what he calls—in a designation that holds both for the past tense of the narrative and for the present tense of the writing—his "favorite sedative" (126/171).

27. No imperative appears more frequently in Beckett's French than this "du calme," which he translates variously in his English versions of his texts. By *Mal vu mal dit* (1981), in which the imperative appears on nearly every sparsely printed page, it will have assumed the status of a basic rhythmic feature, still not quite a rest, but a strong blank beat in all of the restless process of writing.

28. Toward the end of Part I, Molloy describes, in largely mechanical terms, his merciless attack on a "charcoal-burner" whom he holds guilty of desiring his company:

> This is how I went about it. I carefully chose the most favourable position, a few paces from the body, with my back of course turned to it. Then, nicely balanced on my crutches, I began to swing, backwards, forwards . . . I swung,

> that's all that matters, in an ever-widening arc, until I decided the moment had come and launched myself forward with all my strength and consequently, a moment later, backward, which gave the desired result. Where did I get this access of vigour? From my weakness perhaps. (84/113–14)

29. Beckett, *The Unnamable,* 395/181.

30. See Hamm: "The end is in the beginning and yet you go on" (Beckett, *Endgame,* 69/91).

31. Beckett, *The Unnamable,* 291/7.

32. The confusion involved in such scenes is fomented to the point of crystal clarity in *How It Is,* in which the possible subject positions, endlessly juggled in a hopeless attempt to account for the speech that happens there (speech which, even more explicitly than in *The Unnamable,* is a matter of pure quotation) are "tormentor," "victim," and, between the two, "abandoned."

33. Wittgenstein, *Tractatus Logico-Philosophicus,* 6.4311.

34. See again the last lines of *The Unnamable*: "I'll never know, in the silence you don't know, you must go on, I can't go on, I'll go on" (414/213).

35. That Samuel Beckett is unnamable is a paradox: if Samuel Beckett is unnamable then Samuel Beckett is not Samuel Beckett. And that Samuel Beckett is Samuel Beckett is a tautology. The more meaningful claim would be that Samuel Beckett is a Samuel Beckett (a Samuel and a Beckett). "Rose is a rose is a rose is a rose" is not tautological and it wouldn't be even if the second, third, and fourth "roses" were capitalized (Stein, "Sacred Emily," 187). But, by the weird marriage his comedy celebrates, Beckett is also a Molloy.

36. Eliot, "Tradition and the Individual Talent," 50.

37. "What happens when a new work of art is created is something that happens simultaneously to all the works of art which preceded it. The existing monuments form an ideal order among themselves, which is modified by the introduction of the new (the really new) work of art among them . . . Whoever has approved this idea of order, of the form of European, of English literature will not find it preposterous that the past should be altered by the present as much as the present is directed by the past. And the poet who is aware of this will be aware of great difficulties and responsibilities" (Eliot, "Tradition and the Individual Talent," 49–50).

38. Kenner, *The Pound Era,* 141.

39. The first of countless "quaqua" appears on the first page of *How It Is.* "Bits and scraps [*des bribes*]" often follows as in "I have still to say how it was as I hear it in me that was without quaqua on all sides bits and scraps how it was" (51/79). The first "I quote" appears among the speaker's first four words: "how it was I quote before Pim with Pim after Pim how it is three parts I say it as I hear it" (7/9).

Talk of "*bribes*" of language begins in *Molloy*: "On n'invente rien, on croit inventer, s'échapper, on ne fait que balbutier sa leçon, des bribes d'un pensum appris et oublié, la vie sans larmes, telle qu'on la pleure" (41 in the French, 32 in the English). And it becomes frequent in *L'Innommable*. See, for one example among many, the following:

> On lance la voix, elle se perd dans les voûtes, elle appelle ça des voutes, c'est peut-être le firmament, c'est peut-être l'abîme, ce sont des mots, elle parle d'une prison, après tout je veux bien, assez grande pour tout un peuple, pour moi tout seul, ou qui m'attend, je vais y aller, je vais essayer d'y aller, je ne peux pas bouger, j'y suis déjà, je dois y être déjà, si je n'étais pas seul, si tout un peuple y était, et cette voix, la sienne, m'arrivant par bribes (204–5 in the French, 409 in the English)

40. The victim–tormentor [*victime–bourreau*] pairing in *How It Is* develops an old Beckettian idea. Most of the pairings of characters in his theatrical writing take on this form, which he first proposes in 1945 as a description of the respective attitudes of the brothers Bram and Geer van Velde toward what remains to them to paint after having embraced the impossibility of painting, and after having cast off all interest in the *idea* of painting itself:

> There remains, to the one the thing that suffers, the thing that is changed; to the other the thing that inflicts, the thing that effects change.
>
> Two things that, in the detachment in which they might become representable—that of tormentor [*bourreau*] on the one hand and victim on the other—have yet to be created. These are not yet things. That will come. (*Le Monde et le pantalon*, 38–39)

41. Beckett, *How It Is*, 109/169.

FINNEGANS WAKE

1. Joyce, *Finnegans Wake*, 195. I'm taking *How It Is* as a good description of how it is for speakers throughout Beckett's fiction.
2. "Hon! Verg! Nau! Putor! Skam! Scham! Shames!" (*Finnegans Wake*, 93).
3. Shem is to James as Shaun is to John. James Joyce's brother was named John Stanislaus Joyce.
4. The next "word" after Shem's last "quoiq" is the "O" of the beginning of the Anna Livia Plurabelle river chapter. And *Finnegans Wake* ends with the cries of gulls as the Liffey meets the sea:

> We pass through grass brush behush the bush to. Whish! A gull. Gulls. Far calls. Coming far! End here. Us then. Finn, again! Take. Bussoftlhee, mememormee! Till thousendsthee. Lps. The keys to. Given! A way a lone a last a loved a long the (628)

The end of the book is thus echoed, as it is throughout the book, here toward the middle.

5. The shame in this "shamebred music" is born and bred within the family quintet featured in *Finnegans Wake* (HCE, ALP, Shem, Shaun, Issy).

6. See Plato, *Phaedrus,* 275d, e.

7. As in the following examples from *L'Innommable*: "Le dernier pas. Avec quoi? Moi qui n'ai jamais su faire le premier" (78); "Ce n'est pas a moi de juger. Avec quoi jugerais-je?" (108); "A quoi pensais-je? Avec quoi?" (55).

8. Joyce, *Finnegans Wake,* 120. According to Jacques Mercanton, Joyce called upon this concept to defend the seriousness of his book: "[The *Wake*] has to do with an ideal suffering caused by an ideal insomnia," he tells Mercanton. "A sentence in the book describes it in those terms" ("The Hours of James Joyce," 221).

9. In pointing to the "real unrest" that "ideal insomnia" implies, I'm not suggesting that the suffering of "ideal insomnia" is not in fact the "ideal suffering" that Joyce wants it to be (see again Mercanton, "Hours," 221). Though "ideal insomnia" may result in real fatigue, the reader who suffers from it is not *really* suffering, although the masochist can certainly find the pleasure he or she is looking for in the *Wake.* Real suffering is what the real insomniac does when he or she can't sleep.

10. By one hazy account among many, Shem is the writer, in the technical sense, of ALP's letter: "Shem, her penmight" (212). The relationship between the "uttering" and the "writing" of the letter is not at all clear in this account, partly because of the way prepositions swim in it: "Letter, carried of Shaun, son of Hek, written of Shem, brother of Shaun, uttered for Alp, mother of Shem, for Hek, father of Shaun." (420).

11. The review, from 1939, was published under this title in *The New Republic* 91 (July 12). A fuller fleshing-out of this account is published, under the same title, in *The Wound and the Bow.*

12. Levin, "On First Looking into *Finnegans Wake.*" Levin fleshes out this early account in "The Fabulous Artificer," 139–224. Joyce approved particularly of Levin's account (see Ellmann, *James Joyce,* 723).

13. Hart, *Structure and Motif in Finnegans Wake,* 78, 81.

14. Ellman, *James Joyce,* 695–96.

15. Hart, *Structure and Motif,* 99. Hart identifies three principal dream levels in the text: (1) The Dream, the whole of *Finnegans Wake;* (2) the dream of Earwicker, himself a figure of The Dream; and (3) the dream of Shaun, himself a figure within Earwicker's dream.

16. Ibid., 82.

17. Kenner, *Dublin's Joyce,* 17.

18. Ibid., 18.

19. Ibid., 313.

20. Ibid., 301.

21. Attridge, *Joyce Effects*, 133–55.

22. Benstock, *James Joyce*, 152. For his earlier estimation, see *Joyce-Again's Wake: An Analysis of Finnegans Wake.*

23. Bishop, *Joyce's Book of the Dark*, 48 (42–65 for the full argument). Bishop distinguishes "dream-riffed parts of the book from its 'Real Absences'" (47; the term "Real Absence" is taken from page 536 of the *Wake*).

24. For examples of both, see Ellmann, *James Joyce*, 584. Pound's volley voices surprisingly well, considering the source, the most common response to the difficulty of the *Wake*, and, according to Ellmann, it hit Joyce hard. In a letter to Joyce, Pound says, "Up to present I make nothing of it whatever. Nothing so far as I make out, nothing short of divine vision or a new cure for the clapp can possibly be worth all the circumambient peripherization."

25. Ellmann, ed., *Letters of James Joyce*, 146.

26. Ibid., 590, 695.

27. Attridge, *Joyce Effects*, 149.

28. See Ellmann, ed., *Letters of James Joyce*, 537.

29. Joyce, *Finnegans Wake*, 18.

30. Aristotle, *On Generation and Corruption*, 1.2:315b1. The analogy between letters and atoms that Aristotle works through here is essential to ancient atomism, in all of its different schools. According to the analogy, letters are the atoms of language; we can see the invisible atoms of nature through the mirror of language.

31. Aristotle, *De Interpretatione*, 16a1.

32. See Paul K. Saint-Amour, *The Copywrights*, 159–98, for an in-depth study of this tension in Joyce's attitude toward the idea of literary property.

33. Ellmann, *James Joyce*, 6. Quoted from Eugene Jolas's somewhat sycophantic "Homage to the Mythmaker," in *transition* 27 (1938): 174.

34. Or, to follow out this central metaphor of the discourse of the *Wake*, it dissolves in the very saying of it. No homophony is more dear to Joyce's ear than that of "sea" and "say":

> For be all rules of sport 'tis right That youth bedower'd to charm the night Whilst age is dumped to mind the day When wather parted from the say. . . .
>
> From Dancingtree till Suttonstone Theres lads no lie would filch a crown To mull their sack and brew their tay With wather parted from the say. . . .
>
> His bludgeon's broke, his drum is tore. For spuds we'll keep the hat he wore And roll in clover on his clay By wather parted from the say. . . .
>
> To gangstairs strain and anger's up As Hoisty rares the can and cup To speed the bogre's barque away O'er wather parted from the say. (371–73)

35. Clive Hart strongly hears "reverend" in "riverrun" (*Structure and Motif in Finnegans Wake*, 200). Patrick A. McCarthy, who, exploring the close identifica-

tion of the letter with *Finnegans Wake* itself, suggests the ultimate unlimitability of the letter within the *Wake,* hears things in the same way in "Structures and Meanings in *Finnegans Wake,*" 577–78. Sheldon Brivic (*Joyce's Waking Women,* 84) and Jacques Aubert ("riverrun," 77) remark, as well, the "reverend" in "riverrun."

36. By an inverse turn of the same logic that dictates this stretched grammar, "Allgearls is wea" (626).

37. Gillet reports that Joyce said to him something like this:

> Dans *Ulysse,* pour peindre le balbutiement d'une femme qui s'endort, j'avais cherché à finir par le mot le moins fort qu'il m'était possible de découvrir. J'avais trouvé le mot "yes," qui se prononce à peine, qui signifie l'acquiescement, l'abandon, la détente, la fin de toute résistance. Dans le *Work in Progress,* j'ai cherché mieux, si je pouvais. Cette fois, j'ai trouvé le mot le plus glissant, le moins accentué, le plus faible de la langue anglaise, un mot qui n'est même pas un mot, qui sonne à peine entre les dents, un souffle, un rien, l'article *the.* (Ellmann, *Letters of James Joyce,* 712)

38. Here I'm again quoting Beckett's "quaqua on all sides."

39. "A letters," says Issy's (the "wee one's") footnote to this line, "To be slipped on, to be slept by, to be conned to, to be kept up. And when you're done push the chain" —which is to say, "posy cord" (278). In the "letters" of this writing, "pull" becomes "push" or "pos," and though the sense of "pull" pulls the joke, the "pull" of the sending (by flushing) of the scatologized "letters" cannot be given in the "letters" themselves/itself.

40. In chapter I.2, the Cad's wife tells "her particular reverend," in the confidence of confession, what the Cad saw: HCE's "original sin" in Phoenix Park. The reverend then proceeds, of course, to spread the "gossiple":

> Our cad's bit of strife . . . broke of the matter . . . to her particular reverend, the director, whom she had been meaning in her mind primarily to speak with (hosch, intra! Jist a timblespoon!) trusting, between cuppled lips and annie lawrie promises . . . that the gossiple so delivered in his epistolear, buried teatoastally in their Irish stew would go no further than his jesuit's cloth, yet . . . it was this overspoiled priest . . . who, when seized with the facts, was overheard, in his secondary personality . . . to pianissime a slightly varied version of Crookedribs confidentials. (38)

Here too the "reverend" is linked, as a fomenter of rumor, to the "letter." He hears rumors in his "epistolear," which, "buried teatoastally," is, like the "letter" rumored throughout the *Wake,* associated with breakfast, and especially with breakfast tea. To address speech to the ear of this reverend is to address an epistle, as in "Dear . . . Reverend."

41. Ovid, *Metamorphoses,* 269.

42. Ibid., 262.

43. The "s" in "dors" is silent.

AFTERWORD: THE DREAM AND WRITING OF SOCRATES

1. Plato, *Phaedo,* 64c, 80e–81a.

2. Wittgenstein, *Tractatus,* 6.4311.

3. The myth of the cicadas that Socrates recounts in the *Phaedrus* illustrates this way of thinking about music. The cicadas mediate between the mortal world and the muses, telling each muse which human beings have honored her: "and to Calliope, the oldest among them, and Urania, the next after her, who preside over the heavens, and all discourse, human and divine, and sing with the sweetest voice, they report those who honor their special kind of music by leading a philosophical life" (Plato, *Phaedrus,* 259d). The cicadas are the metamorphic remains of an ancient people "so overwhelmed with the pleasure of singing" that "they died without even realizing it" (259 b, c).

4. Plato, *Phaedrus,* 276a.

5. Ibid., 275d, e.

6. Coins for Charon, the ferryman.

7. "If you don't know how to die, don't worry; Nature will tell you what to do on the spot, fully and adequately. She will do this job perfectly for you; don't bother your head about it . . . A quarter of an hour of suffering, without consequence, without harm, does not deserve any particular precepts. To tell the truth, we prepare ourselves against the preparations for death. Philosophy orders us to have death ever before our eyes, to foresee and consider it before our time comes, and afterward gives us the rules and precautions to provide against our being wounded by this foresight and this thought. That is what those doctors do who make us ill so that they may have something on which to employ their drugs and their art" (*Of Physiognomy,* 804).

8. Plato, *Phaedo,* 61d, e.

9. See again Plato, *Phaedrus,* 276a.

10. This is not to say that all of those present on the scene are perfectly calm. When Socrates finally drinks the poison—when the dialogue reaches its outer limit—most of those present begin to weep. But Socrates stops them instantly: "What is this? . . . It is mainly for this reason that I sent the women away" (117d, e). The dialogue begins with Socrates' banishment of Xanthippe—his wife, who's upset—from the scene (60a, b). Like Evenus, Xanthippe gives voice to some disquiet in the face of death, but where Evenus' question on writing gets considered in his absence—in writing, as it were—Xanthippe is completely excluded from the process of questioning. The very completeness of this exclusion marks it as arbitrary. Where Socrates' treatment of Evenus is artfully ironic, his treatment of Xanthippe is simply unfair. Evenus is anxious,

and anxious about his own death. Xanthippe is sad, and sad about Socrates' death. While the philosopher's calm and Evenus' anxiety are linked closely in an economy, there's no indication that Xanthippe's sadness has anything essentially to do with Socrates' calm, and there's no philosophical reason not to recognize its dignity. Socrates is philosophically obligated not to be sad about his own death, but he is not philosophically obligated not to empathize with the sadness of those who are losing him. Had Xanthippe been present for the dialogue, she might have sharpened Socrates' sense of his obligation to his dream. That sense is at its dullest in his dismissal of her.

11. Perhaps Plato was not so much ill as upset about Socrates' death (see, again, the *Phaedo*, 59b).

SELECTED BIBLIOGRAPHY

Abbott, H. Porter. *Beckett Writing Beckett: The Author in the Autograph.* Ithaca: Cornell University Press, 1996.

Adorno, Theodor W. "Trying to Understand *Endgame.*" In *Notes to Literature.* Vol. 1. Trans. Shierry Weber Nicholsen. New York: Columbia University Press, 1991.

Arendt, Hannah. *The Human Condition.* Chicago: University of Chicago Press, 1958.

Aristotle. *De Interpretatione.* In *The Complete Works of Aristotle.* Vol. 1. Ed. Jonathan Barnes. Princeton: Princeton University Press, 1984.

———. *On Divination in Sleep.* In *The Complete Works of Aristotle.* Vol. 1. Ed. Jonathan Barnes. Princeton: Princeton University Press, 1984.

———. *On Dreams.* In *The Complete Works of Aristotle.* Vol. 1. Ed. Jonathan Barnes. Princeton: Princeton University Press, 1984.

———. *On Generation and Corruption.* In *The Complete Works of Aristotle.* Vol. 1. Ed. Jonathan Barnes. Princeton: Princeton University Press, 1984.

———. *On Sleep.* In *The Complete Works of Aristotle.* Vol. 1. Ed. Jonathan Barnes. Princeton: Princeton University Press, 1984.

Artemidorus. *Oneirocritica.* Trans. Robert J. White. Park Ridge: Noyes Press, 1975.

Attridge, Derek. *Joyce Effects: On Language, Theory, and History.* Cambridge: Cambridge University Press, 2000.

———. *Peculiar Language: Literature as Difference from the Renaissance to James Joyce.* Ithaca: Cornell University Press, 1988.

Aubert, Jacques. "riverrun." In *Post-Structuralist Joyce.* Eds. Derek Attridge and Daniel Ferrer. Cambridge: Cambridge University Press, 1984.

Badiou, Alain. *Beckett: L'Increvable désir.* Paris: Hachette, 1995.

———. *L'Être et l'événement.* Paris: Seuil, 1988.

Bailey, Cyril. *The Greek Atomists and Epicurus.* Oxford: Oxford University Press, 1928.

Bair, Deirdre. *Samuel Beckett, A Biography*. New York: Harcourt Brace Jovanovich, 1990.
Bakhtin, Mikhail. "Discourse in the Novel." In *The Dialogic Imagination*. Ed. Michael Holquist. Austin: University of Texas Press, 1981.
Bal, Mieke. "Mise en abyme et iconicité." *Littérature* 29 (February 1978).
Banfield, Ann. *Unspeakable Sentences: Narration and representation in the language of fiction*. Boston: Routledge, 1982.
Barthes, Roland. *Le degré zéro de l'écriture*. Paris: Seuil, 1953.
Bataille, Georges. "Le silence de Molloy." *Critique*, tome vii, no. 48 (May 1951).
Beckett, Samuel. *Catastrophe et autres dramaticules*. Paris: Minuit, 1982.
———. *Comment c'est*. Paris: Minuit, 1961.
———. *Company*. London: Calder, 1980.
———. *The Complete Short Prose*. New York: Grove Press, 1995.
———. *Dream of Fair to Middling Women*. Dublin: The Black Cat Press, 1992.
———. *En attendant Godot*. Paris: Minuit, 1952.
———. *Endgame*. New York: Grove Press, 1958.
———. *Fin de partie*. Paris: Minuit, 1957.
———. *How It Is*. New York: Grove, 1964.
———. *L'Innommable*. Paris: Minuit, 1953.
———. *Krapp's Last Tape and Other Dramatic Pieces*. New York: Grove Press, 1958.
———. *Malone Dies*. In *Three Novels*. New York: Grove Press, 1958.
———. *Malone meurt*. Paris: Minuit, 1951.
———. *Mal vu mal dit*. Paris: Minuit, 1981.
———. *Mercier et Camier*. Paris: Minuit, 1970.
———. *Molloy*. Paris: Minuit, 1951.
———. *Molloy*. In *Three Novels*. New York: Grove Press, 1958.
———. *Le monde et le pantalon* suivi de *Peintres de l'empêchement*. Paris: Minuit, 1990.
———. *More Pricks than Kicks*. New York: Grove, 1972
———. *Nouvelles et textes pour rien*. Paris: Minuit, 1958.
———. *Oh les beaux jours*. Paris: Minuit, 1963.
———. *Proust*. In *Proust and Three Dialogues*. London: Calder, 1965.
———. *Quad et autres pièces pour la télévision*. Paris: Minuit, 1992.
———. *The Unnamable*. In *Three Novels*. New York: Grove Press, 1958.
———. *Watt*. New York: Grove Press, 1953.
Beckett, Samuel and Georges Duthuit. *Three Dialogues*. In *Proust and Three Dialogues*. London: Calder, 1965.
———. *Trois dialogues*. Paris: Minuit, 1998.
Begnal, Michael H. *Dreamscheme: Narrative and Voice in* Finnegans Wake. Syracuse: Syracuse University Press, 1988.
Béguin, Albert. *L'Ame romantique et le rêve*. Paris: José Corti, 1991.
Benjamin, Walter. *The Arcades Project*. Trans. Howard Eiland and Kevin McLaughlin. Cambridge: Harvard University Press, 1999.

Benstock, Bernard. *James Joyce.* New York: Frederick Unger, 1985.

———. *Joyce-Again's Wake: An Analysis of* Finnegans Wake. Seattle: University of Washington Press, 1965.

Bersani, Leo. *Balzac to Beckett: Center and Circumference in French Fiction.* New York: Oxford University Press, 1970.

———. *The Death of Stéphane Mallarmé.* Cambridge: Cambridge University Press, 1982.

Bersani, Leo and Ulysse Dutoit. *Arts of Impoverishment: Beckett, Rothko, Resnais.* Cambridge: Harvard University Press, 1993.

Bishop, John. *Joyce's Book of the Dark:* Finnegans Wake. Madison: The University of Wisconsin Press, 1986.

Blanchot, Maurice. *The Book to Come.* Trans. Charlotte Mandell. Stanford: Stanford University Press, 2003.

———. *La Communauté inavouable.* Paris: Minuit, 1983.

———. "Dreaming, Writing." In *Friendship.* Trans. Elizabeth Rottenberg. Stanford: Stanford University Press, 1997.

———. *L'Écriture du désastre.* Paris: Gallimard, 1980.

———. *L'Entretien infini.* Paris: Gallimard, 1969.

———. *L'Espace littéraire.* Paris: Gallimard, 1955.

———. *The Infinite Conversation.* Trans. Susan Hanson. Minneapolis: University of Minnesota Press, 1993.

———. *Lautréamont and Sade.* Trans. Stuart and Michelle Kendall. Stanford: Stanford University Press, 2004.

———. *Lautréamont et Sade.* Paris: Minuit, 1963.

———. *Le Livre à venir.* Paris: Gallimard, 1959.

———. "Rêver, Écrire." In *L'Amitié.* Paris: Gallimard, 1971

———. *The Space of Literature.* Trans. Ann Smock. Lincoln: University of Nebraska Press, 1982.

———. *The Unavowable Community.* Trans. Pierre Joris. Barrytown, NY: Station Hill Press, 1988.

———. *The Writing of the Disaster.* Trans. Ann Smock. Lincoln: University of Nebraska Press, 1995.

Bond, Gerald A. ed. *The Poetry of William VII, Count of Poitiers, IX Duke of Aquitaine.* New York and London: Garland, 1982.

Borch-Jacobsen, Mikkel. *The Freudian Subject.* Trans. Catherine Porter. Stanford: Stanford University Press, 1988.

Braet, Herman. "Rêve, réalité, écriture." In *I sogni nel medioevo.* Ed. Tullio Gregory. Rome: Edizioni dell'Ateneo, 1985.

Breton, André. *Manifestes du surréalisme.* Paris: Gallimard, 1987.

Brivic, Sheldon. *Joyce's Waking Women: An Introduction to* Finnegans Wake. Madison: University of Wisconsin Press, 1995.

Burnyeat, Myles, ed. *The Skeptical Tradition.* Berkeley: University of California Press, 1983.
Cadava, Eduardo, Peter Connor, and Jean-Luc Nancy, eds. *Who Comes After the Subject?* New York: Routledge, 1991.
Caillois, Roger. *Approches de l'imaginaire.* Paris: Gallimard, 1974.
———. *L'Incertitude qui vient des rêves.* Paris: Gallimard, 1956.
———. *Obliques précédé de Images, images.* Paris: Editions Stock, 1975.
Caillois, Roger and G. E. von Grunebaum, eds. *Le rêve et les sociétés humaines.* Paris: Gallimard, 1967.
Calderón de la Barca, Pedro. *La vida es sueño.* Ed. Ciriaco Morón Arroyo. Madrid: Ediciones Cátedra, 1992.
Cavell, Stanley. *The Claim of Reason.* Oxford: Oxford University Press, 1979.
———. *Must We Mean What We Say?* New York: Scribner's, 1969.
Cervantes, Miguel de. *Don Quijote de la Mancha.* Ed. Martín de Riquer. 12th ed. 2 vols. Barcelona: Editorial Juventud, 1955.
———. *Don Quixote.* Trans. Edith Grossman. New York: Harper Collins, 2003.
Cohn, Ruby. *Samuel Beckett: The Comic Gamut.* New Brunswick: Rutgers University Press, 1962.
Connor, Steven. *Samuel Beckett: Repetition, Theory, and Text.* Oxford: Basil Blackwell, 1988.
Culler, Jonathan. *Framing the Sign.* Norman: University of Oklahoma Press, 1988.
Dällenbach, Lucien. *Le récit spéculaire.* Paris: Seuil, 1977.
Dante. *Purgatorio.* Trans. Allen Mandelbaum. New York: Bantam Classic, 1984.
Dastur, Françoise. *La mort: essai sur la finitude.* Paris: Hatier, 1994.
de Lattre, Alain. *L'Occasionalisme d'Arnold Geulincx, étude sur la constitution de la doctrine.* Paris: Minuit, 1967.
Deleuze, Gilles. "Le cerveau, c'est l'écran." *Cahiers du Cinéma* (March 1986).
———. *Difference and Repetition.* Trans. Paul Patton. New York: Columbia University Press, 1994.
———. *Différence et répétition.* Paris: Presses Universitaires de France, 1972.
———. *L'Image-mouvement.* Paris: Minuit, 1983.
Deleuze, Gilles and Félix Guattari. *L'Anti-Oedipe.* Paris: Minuit, 1972.
———. *Mille plateaux.* Paris: Minuit, 1980.
de Man, Paul. *Aesthetic Ideology.* Minneapolis: University of Minnesota Press, 1996.
———. *Allegories of Reading: Figural Language in Rousseau, Nietzsche, Rilke, and Proust.* New Haven, CT: Yale University Press, 1979.
———. *The Resistance to Theory.* Minneapolis, MN: University of Minnesota Press, 1986.
———. *The Rhetoric of Romanticism.* New York: Columbia University Press, 1984.
Derrida, Jacques. *Apories: mourir—s'attendre aux "limites de la vérité."* Paris: Galilée, 1996.

———. *De la grammatologie.* Paris: Minuit, 1967
———. *La Dissémination.* Paris: Seuil, 1972.
———. *L'Écriture et la différence.* Paris: Seuil, 1967.
———. "Freud and the Scene of Writing." In *Writing and Difference.* Trans. Alan Bass. Chicago: University of Chicago Press, 1978.
———. *Marges de la Philosophie.* Paris: Minuit, 1972.
———. *Of Grammatology.* Trans. Gayatri Spivak. Baltimore: Johns Hopkins University Press, 1976.
———. *Parages.* Paris: Galilée, 1986.
———. "Signature, Event, Context." In *Margins of Philosophy.* Trans. Alan Bass. Chicago: University of Chicago Press, 1982.
Descartes, René. *Meditations on First Philosophy.* Trans. Donald A. Cress. Indianapolis: Hackett, 1993.
Dodds, E. R. *The Greeks and the Irrational.* Berkeley: University of California Press, 1964.
Ducat, Philippe. "Le sujet du rêve: présentation de la correspondance Husserl/Héring." *Alter: Revue de Phénomenologie* no.5 (1997).
Dumont, Jean-Paul. *Les sceptiques grecs.* Paris: PUF, 1966.
———. *Le scepticisme et le phénomène.* Paris: Vrin, 1972.
Dunlop, Charles E. M., ed. *Philosophical Essays on Dreaming.* Ithaca: Cornell University Press, 1977.
Eliot, George. *Middlemarch.* Norton Critical Edition. Ed. Bert G. Hornback. NY: Norton, 2000.
Eliot, T. S. "Tradition and the Individual Talent." In *The Sacred Wood.* London: Methuen, 1950.
Ellmann, Richard. *James Joyce.* New York: Oxford University Press, 1982.
———, ed. *Letters of James Joyce.* Vol. III. New York: The Viking Press, 1966.
Éluard, Paul. *Poésie ininterrompue.* Paris: Gallimard, 1946.
Empson, William. *Some Versions of Pastoral.* New York: New Directions, 1974.
Foucault, Michel. *Histoire de la sexualité III: Le souci de soi.* Paris: Gallimard, 1984.
———. "Introduction." Ludwig Binswanger. *Le rêve et l'existence.* Paris: Desclée de Brouwer, 1954.
Freud, Sigmund. *Beyond the Pleasure Principle.* Trans. James Strachey. New York: Norton, 1961.
———. *The Claims of Psycho-Analysis to Scientific Interest.* Trans. James Strachey. Standard Edition. Vol. xiii. London: Hogarth Press, 1953.
———. "Dora." In *Case Histories I.* Trans. James Strachey. London: Penguin, 1990.
———. *Dreams and Telepathy.* Trans. James Strachey. Standard Edition. Vol. xviii. London: Hogarth Press.
———.*The Interpretation of Dreams.* Trans. James Strachey. New York: Avon Books, 1965.

———. *Introductory Lectures on Psychoanalysis.* Trans. James Strachey. Standard Edition. Vol. xv. London: Hogarth Press.

———. *Jokes and Their Relation to the Unconscious.* Trans. James Strachey. Standard Edition. Vol. viii. London: Hogarth Press.

———. *A Metapsychological Supplement to the Theory of Dreams.* Trans. James Strachey. Standard Edition. Vol. xiv. London: Hogarth Press.

———. *New Introductory Lectures on Psychoanalysis.* Trans. James Strachey. London: Norton, 1964.

———. *An Outline of Psychoanalysis.* Trans. James Strachey. Standard Edition. Vol. xxiii. London: Hogarth Press.

———. *Remarks on the Theory and Practice of Dream-Interpretation.* Trans. James Strachey. Standard Edition. Vol. xix. London: Hogarth Press.

———. *Some Additional Notes on Dream-Interpretation as a Whole.* Trans. James Strachey. Standard Edition. Vol. xix. London: Hogarth Press.

———. *Die Traumdeutung.* Gesammelte Werke, vols. ii and iii. London: Imago Publishing, 1942.

———. "The Wolf Man." In *Case Histories II.* Trans. James Strachey. London: Penguin, 1991.

García Lorca, Federico. *Así que pasen cinco años.* Ed. E. F. Granell. Madrid: Taurus, 1976.

Gasché, Rodolphe. *The Tain of the Mirror: Derrida and the Philosophy of Reflection.* Cambridge: Harvard University Press, 1986.

Genette, Gérard. *Figures III.* Paris: Seuil, 1966.

———. *Nouveau discours du récit.* Paris: Seuil, 1983.

Glasheen, Adaline. *Third Census of Finnegans Wake: An Index of the Characters and Their Roles.* Berkeley: University of California Press, 1977.

Goldin, Frederick, trans. *Lyrics of the Troubadours and Trouvères: An Anthology and a History.* Gloucester: Peter Smith, 1983.

Góngora, Luis de. *Las soledades.* Madrid: Sociedad de Estudios y Publicaciones, 1956.

Gontarski, S. E. *The Intent of Undoing in Samuel Beckett's Dramatic Texts.* Bloomington: Indiana University Press, 1985.

Gray, Thomas. *The Complete English Poems.* Ed. James Reeves. London: Heinemann, 1973.

Gregory, Tullio, ed. *I sogni nel medioevo.* Rome: Edizioni dell'Ateneo, 1985.

Guillory, John. *Cultural Capital: The Problem of Literary Canon Formation.* Chicago: University of Chicago Press, 1993.

Hansen, Mark B. N. *Embodying Technesis: Technology Beyond Writing.* Ann Arbor: University of Michigan Press, 2000.

Hart, Clive. *Structure and Motif in Finnegans Wake.* Chicago: Northwestern University Press, 1962.

Hayman, David. *Joyce et Mallarmé: stylistique de la suggestion.* Paris: Lettres Modernes, 1956.
Hayman, David and Sam Slote, eds. *Probes: Genetic Studies in Joyce.* European Joyce Studies 5. Amsterdam: Rodopi, 1995.
Heidegger, Martin. *Being and Time.* Trans. John Macquarrie and Edward Robinson. San Francisco: Harper and Row, 1962.
Husserl, Edmund. *La terre ne se meut pas.* Trans. Didier Franck. Paris: Minuit, 1989.
Jefferson, Ann. "*Mise en abyme* and the Prophetic in Narrative." *Style* 17, no.2 (Spring 1983).
Johnson, Barbara. *The Feminist Difference.* Cambridge: Harvard University Press, 1998.
Joyce, James. *Chamber Music.* New York: Columbia University Press, 1954.
———. *Dubliners.* New York: Viking, 1967.
———. *Exiles.* London: J. Cape, 1936.
———. *Finnegans Wake.* London: Faber and Faber, 1939.
———. *Giacomo Joyce.* New York: Viking, 1968.
———. *The Letters of James Joyce.* Vol. iii. Ed. Richard Ellmann. New York: Viking, 1966.
———. *Pomes penyeach.* London: Faber and Faber, 1933.
———. *A Portrait of the Artist as a Young Man.* New York: Viking, 1964.
———. *Stephen Hero.* London: Ace Books, 1961.
———. *Ulysses.* New York: Vintage, 1961.
Keats, John. *The Poems of John Keats.* Ed. Jack Stillinger. Cambridge: Harvard University Press, 1978
Kenner, Hugh. *Dublin's Joyce.* London: Chatto and Windus, 1955.
———. *Flaubert, Joyce, and Beckett: The Stoic Comedians.* Boston: Beacon Press, 1962.
———. *Joyce's Voices.* Berkeley: University of California Press, 1978.
———. *The Mechanic Muse.* New York: Oxford University Press, 1987.
———. "Man in the Room." In *Samuel Beckett: A Critical Study.* Berkeley: University of California Press, 1961.
———. *The Pound Era.* Berkeley: University of California Press, 1971.
———. *A Reader's Guide to Samuel Beckett.* New York: Farrar, Strauss, and Giroux, 1973.
Kittler, Friedrich A. *Discourse Networks 1800/1900.* Trans. Michael Metteer. Stanford: Stanford University Press, 1990.
Knowlson, James. *Damned to Fame: The Life of Samuel Beckett.* London: Bloomsbury, 1996.
Lacan, Jacques. *Écrits I.* Paris: Seuil, 1966.
———. *Écrits II.* Paris: Seuil, 1966.
———. *Le Séminaire, Livre i: Les écrits techniques de Freud.* Paris: Seuil, 1975.

———. *Le Séminaire, Livre ii: Le moi dans la théorie de Freud et dans la technique de la psychanalyse.* Paris: Seuil, 1978.

———. *Le Séminaire, Livre v: Les formations de l'inconscient.* Paris: Seuil, 1998.

———. *Le Séminaire, Livre vii: L'ethique de la psychanalyse.* Paris: Seuil, 1986.

———. *Le Séminaire, Livre xi: Les quatre concepts fondamentaux de la psychanalyse.* Paris: Seuil, 1973.

Lacoue-Labarthe, Philippe. *Typography: Mimesis, Philosophy, Politics.* Stanford: Stanford University Press, 1998.

Laporte, Roger. *La Veille.* Paris: Gallimard, 1963.

Lautréamont. *Oeuvres Complètes.* Paris: Librairie José Corti, 1946.

Levin, Harry. "The Fabulous Artificer." In *James Joyce: A Critical Introduction.* New York: New Directions, 1960.

———. "On First Looking Into *Finnegans Wake.*" *New Directions in Prose and Poetry* 4 (1939).

Levinas, Emmanuel. *L'au-delà du verset.* Minuit: 1982.

———. *De l'existence à l'existent.* Paris: Vrin, 1984.

———. *Existence and Existents.* Trans. Alphonso Lingis. Dordrecht: Kluwer, 1988.

———. *Totalité et infini: essai sur l'extériorité.* The Hague: M. Nijhoff, 1961.

Lewis, Pericles. "The Modern Novelist as Redeemer of the Nation." In *Modernism, Nationalism, and the Novel.* Cambridge: Cambridge University Press, 2000.

Lucretius. *De rerum natura, libri sex.* Ed. and trans. Cyril Bailey. Oxford: Oxford University Press, 1947.

Lyotard, Jean-François. "The Dream-Work Does not Think." In Andrew Benjamin, ed. *The Lyotard Reader.* Oxford: Basil Blackwell, 1989.

Macrobius. *Commentary on the Dream of Scipio.* Trans. William Harris Stahl. New York: Columbia, 1952.

Mahaffey, Vicki. *Reauthorizing Joyce.* Cambridge: Cambridge University Press, 1988.

Malcolm, Norman. *Dreaming.* New York: Humanities Press, 1959.

———. "Dreaming and Skepticism." In *Philosophical Essays on Dreaming.* Ed. Charles E. M. Dunlop. Ithaca, NY: Cornell University Press, 1977.

Mallarmé, Stéphane. *Igitur; Divagations; Un coup de dés.* Paris: Gallimard, 1976.

McCarthy, Patrick A. "Structures and Meanings in *Finnegans Wake.*" In *A Companion to Joyce Studies.* Ed. Zach Bowen and James F. Carens. London: Greenwood Press, 1984.

McHale, Brian. "Free Indirect Discourse: A Survey of Recent Accounts." *PTL* 3, no.2, (April 1978).

———. *Postmodernist Fiction.* London: Methuen, 1987.

———. "Unspeakable Sentences, Unnatural Acts: Linguistics and Poetics Revisited." *Poetics Today* 4:1 (1983).

McGann, Jerome. *Black Riders: The Visible Language of Modernism.* Princeton: Princeton University Press, 1993.

Mercanton, Jacques. "The Hours of James Joyce." In *Portraits of the Artist in Exile: Recollections of James Joyce by Europeans.* Ed. Willard Potts. Trans. Lloyd C. Parks. Seattle: University of Washington Press, 1979.

Milner, Jean-Claude. *L'Amour de la langue.* Paris: Seuil, 1978.

Milton, John. *Complete Poems and Major Prose.* Ed. Merritt Y. Hughes. New York: The Odyssey Press, 1957.

Montaigne, Michel de. *The Complete Essays of Montaigne.* Trans. Donald M. Frame. Stanford: Stanford University Press, 1958.

———. *Oeuvres completes.* Eds. Albert Thibaudet and Maurice Rat. Paris: Gallimard, 1962.

Moyal, Georges J. D. *La critique cartésienne de la raison: folie, rêve et liberté dans les méditations.* Paris: Vrin, 1997.

Norris, Margot. *The Decentered Universe of* Finnegans Wake: *A Structuralist Analysis.* Baltimore: Johns Hopkins University Press, 1976.

Ovid. *Metamorphoses.* Trans. Mary M. Innes. London: Penguin, 1955.

Pasolini, Pier Paulo. "Sur le discours indirect libre." In *L'expérience hérétique: langue et cinéma.* Paris: Payot, 1976.

Pessoa, Fernando. *The Book of Disquietude.* Trans. Richard Zenith. Manchester: Carcanet, 1996.

Plato. *Apology.* In *Complete Works.* Ed. John M. Cooper. Trans. G. M. A. Grube. Indianapolis: Hackett, 1997.

———. *Crito.* In *Complete Works.* Ed. John M. Cooper. Trans. G. M. A. Grube. Indianapolis: Hackett, 1997.

———. *Phaedo.* In *Complete Works.* Ed. John M. Cooper. Trans. G. M. A. Grube. Indianapolis: Hackett, 1997.

———. *Phaedrus.* In *Complete Works.* Ed. John M. Cooper. Trans. Alexander Nehamas and Paul Woodruff. Indianapolis: Hackett, 1997.

———. *Republic.* In *Complete Works.* Ed. John M. Cooper. Trans. G. M. A. Grube, rev. C. D. C Reeve. Indianapolis: Hackett, 1997.

Pilling, John, ed. *Beckett's Dream Notebook.* Reading: Beckett International Foundation, 1999.

Pontalis, J. B. *Entre le rêve et la douleur.* Paris: Gallimard, 1977.

Rabaté, Dominique. *Poétiques de la voix.* Paris: Librairie José Corti, 1999.

———. *Le roman français depuis 1900.* Paris: PUF, 1998.

———. *Vers une littérature de l'épuisement.* Paris: José Corti, 1991.

Rabaté, Jean-Michel. *James Joyce and the Politics of Egoism.* Cambridge: Cambridge University Press, 2001.

———. *Joyce Upon the Void: The Genesis of Doubt.* London: Macmillan, 1991.

Rabaté, Jean-Michel, ed. *Beckett avant Beckett: essais sur le jeune Beckett (1930–1945).* Paris: Presses de l'Ecole Normale Supérieure, 1984.

Rainey, Lawrence. *Institutions of Modernism: Literary Elites and Public Culture.* New Haven: Yale University Press, 1998.

Saint-Amour, Paul K. *The Copywrights: Intellectual Property and the Literary Imagination.* Ithaca: Cornell University Press, 2003.

Senn, Fritz and Michael H. Begnal, ed. *A Conceptual Guide to* Finnegans Wake. University Park: Penn State University Press, 1974.

Shakespeare, William. *Richard III.* In *The Riverside Shakespeare.* General ed. G. Blakemore Evans. Boston: Houghton Mifflin, 1997.

Sor Juana Inés de la Cruz. *Primero sueno.* In Georgina Sabat de Rivers and Elias L. Rivers, ed. *Obras selectas.* Barcelona: Noguer, 1976.

Starobinski, Jean. "Acheronta Movebo" In *The Trials of Psychoanalysis.* Ed. Françoise Meltzer. Chicago: The University of Chicago Press, 1987.

Stein, Gertrude. "Sacred Emily." In *Geography and Plays.* Madison: University of Wisconsin Press, 1993.

Tedlock, Barbara, ed. *Dreaming: Anthropological and Psychological Interpretations.* Cambridge: Cambridge University Press, 1987.

Tindall, William York. *A Reader's Guide to* Finnegans Wake. Syracuse: Syracuse University Press, 1969.

Todorov, Tzvetan. "L'Espoir chez Beckett." *Revue d'Esthétique,* h.s. (1986).

Vico, Giambattista. *New Science.* London: Penguin, 1999.

Wahl, Jean. *1848–1948: Cent années de l'histoire de l'idée d'existence.* Paris: Centre de Documentation Universitaire, 1949.

Wilson, Edmund. "The Dream of H. C. Earwicker." In *The Wound and the Bow.* New York: Oxford University Press, 1947.

Wittgenstein, Ludwig. *Lectures and Conversations on Aesthetics, Psychology, and Religious Belief.* Ed. Cyril Barrett. Berkeley: University of California Press, 1966.

———. *Philosophical Investigations.* Trans. G. E. M. Anscombe. Oxford: Basil Blackwell, 1967.

———. *Tractatus Logico-Philosophicus.* Trans. C. K. Ogden. London: Routledge, 1922.

Zizek, Slavoj. *The Sublime Object of Ideology.* London: Verso, 1989.

INDEX